Pavilion Press

HOMELAND SECURITY

US NATIONAL SECURITY STRATEGY

Office of Homeland Security

PAVILION PRESS

Philadelphia

Pavilion Press, Inc.

Philadelphia • New York •

Homeland Security, US National Security Strategy
Office of Homeland Security

ISBN: .

| | Paperback | 1-4145-0338-5 |
| | Hard Cover | 1-4145-0314-8 |

This book is printed on acid-free paper. Designed for readability

Library of Congress

Cataloging-in-Publication Data

1. Homeland Security • 2. United States •
3. Terrorism 4. American History • 5. Intelligence

Composition by Pavilion Press, Inc. Philadelphia, PA www.pavilionpress.com

Pavilion Press offers a range of fine art reproductions, posters, as well as note, greeting and playing cards based on the original cover art and illustrations from its extensive collections.

* * *

* * *

For a complete list of authors, titles, special offers, discounts and future products visit

www.pavilionpress.com.

Acknowledgements

This is a reproduction, with minor changes, of the July 2002 report of the Office of Homeland Security.

Introduction

LETTER FROM PRESIDENT GEORGE W. BUSH:

July 2 0 0 2

My fellow Americans:

Since September 11, 2001, our Nation has taken great strides to improve homeland security. Citizens, industry, and government leaders from across the political spectrum have cooperated to a degree rarely seen in American history. Congress has passed important laws that have strengthened the ability of our law enforcement agencies to investigate and prosecute terrorists and those who support them. We have formed a global coalition that has defeated terrorists and their supporters in Afghanistan and other parts of the world. More than 60,000 American troops are deployed around the world in the war on terrorism. We have strengthened our aviation security and tightened our borders. We have stockpiled medicines to defend against bioterrorism and improved our ability to combat weapons of mass destruction. We have improved information sharing among our intelligence agencies, and we have taken important steps to protect our critical infrastructure. We are today a Nation at risk to a new and changing threat. The terrorist threat to America takes many forms, has many places to hide, and is often invisible. Yet the need for homeland security is not tied solely to today's terrorist threat. The need for homeland security is tied to our enduring vulnerability. Terrorists wish to attack us and exploit our vulnerabilities because of the freedoms we hold dear.

The U.S. government has no more important mission than protecting the homeland from future terrorist attacks. Yet the country has never had a comprehensive and shared vision of how best to achieve this goal. On October 8, I established the Office of Homeland Security within the White House and, as its first responsibility, directed it to produce the first *National Strategy for Homeland Security*.

The *National Strategy for Homeland Security* is the product of more than eight months of intense consultation across the United States. My Administration has talked to literally thousands of people–governors and mayors, state legislators and Members of Congress, concerned citizens and foreign leaders, professors and soldiers, firefighters and police officers, doctors and scientists, airline pilots and farmers, business leaders and civic activists, journalists and veterans, and the victims and their families.We have listened carefully. This is a national strategy, not a federal strategy. We must rally our entire society to overcome a new and very complex challenge. Homeland security is a shared responsibility. In addition to a national strategy, we need compatible, the white house washington mutually supporting state, local, and private-sector strategies. Individual volunteers must channel their energy and commitment in support of the national and local strategies. My intent in publishing the *National Strategy for Homeland Security* is to help Americans achieve a shared cooperation in the area of homeland security for years to come. The *Strategy* seeks to do so by answering four basic questions:

• What is "homeland security" and what missions does it entail?

• What do we seek to accomplish, and what are the most important goals of homeland security?

• What is the federal executive branch doing now to accomplish these goals and what should it do in the future?

• What should non-federal governments, the private sector, and citizens do to help secure the homeland?

The *National Strategy for Homeland Security* is a beginning. It calls for bold and necessary steps. It creates a comprehensive plan for using America's talents and resources to enhance our protection and reduce our vulnerability to terrorist attacks.We have produced a comprehensive national strategy that is based on the principles of cooperation and partnership. As a result of this *Strategy*, firefighters will be better equipped to fight fires, police officers better armed to fight crime, businesses better able to protect their data and information systems, and scientists better able to fight Mother Nature's deadliest diseases.We will not achieve these goals overnight… but we will achieve them. Our enemy is smart and resolute.We are smarter and more resolute.We will prevail against all who believe they can stand in the way of America's commitment to freedom, liberty, and our way of life.

GEORGE W. BUSH

THE WHITE HOUSE

July 16, 2002

Table of Contents

ILLUSTRATIONS

Countless places in the nation are vulnerable to attack.

We must use intelligence and science to protect ourselves.

Destruction of key assets could compromise the nation.

Priorities must both protect and respect our laws and liberties.

Strategies include prevention and recovery.

CHAPTER 1
Rationale and Summary

This document is the first *National Strategy for Homeland Security*. The purpose of the *Strategy* is to mobilize and organize our Nation to secure the U.S. homeland from terrorist attacks. This is an exceedingly complex mission that requires coordinated and focused effort from our entire society—the federal government, state and local governments, the private sector, and the American people.1

People and organizations all across the United States have taken many steps to improve our security since the September 11 attacks, but a great deal of work remains. The *National Strategy for Homeland Security* will help to prepare our Nation for the work ahead in several ways. It provides direction to the federal government departments and agencies that have a role in homeland security. It suggests steps that state and local governments, private companies and organizations, and individual Americans can take to improve our security and offers incentives for them to do so. It recommends certain actions to the Congress. In this way, the *Strategy* provides a framework for the contributions that we all can make to secure our homeland.

The *National Strategy for Homeland Security* is the beginning of what will be a long struggle to protect our Nation from terrorism. It establishes a foundation upon which to organize our efforts and provides initial guidance to prioritize the work ahead. The *Strategy* will be adjusted and amended over time.We must be prepared to adapt as our enemies in the war on terrorism alter their means of attack.

Strategic Objectives

The strategic objectives of homeland security in order of priority are to:

- Prevent terrorist attacks within the United States;

- Reduce America's vulnerability to terrorism; and

- Minimize the damage and recover from attacks that do occur.

Threat and Vulnerability

Unless we act to prevent it, a new wave of terrorism, potentially involving the world's most destructive weapons, looms in America's future. It is a challenge as formidable as any ever faced by our Nation. But we are not daunted. We possess the determination and the resources to defeat our enemies and secure our homeland against the threats they pose. One fact dominates all homeland security threat assessments: terrorists are strategic actors. They choose their targets deliberately based on the weaknesses they observe in our defenses and our preparedness. We must defend ourselves against a wide range of means and methods of attack. Our enemies are working to obtain chemical, biological, radiological, and nuclear weapons for the purpose of wreaking unprecedented damage on America. Terrorists continue to employ conventional means of attack, while at the same time gaining expertise in less traditional means, such as cyber attacks. Our society presents an almost infinite array of potential targets that can be attacked through a variety of methods.

Our enemies seek to remain invisible, lurking in the shadows. We are actively engaged in uncovering them. Al-Qaeda remains America's most immediate and serious threat despite our success in disrupting its network in Afghanistan and elsewhere. Other international terrorist organizations, as well as domestic terrorist groups, possess the will and capability to attack the United States.

Organizing for a Secure Homeland

In response to the homeland security challenge facing us, the President has proposed, and the Congress is presently considering, the most extensive reorganization of the federal government in the past fifty years. The establishment of a new Department of Homeland Security would ensure greater accountability over critical homeland security missions and unity of purpose among the agencies responsible for them.2 American democracy is rooted in the precepts of federalism — a system of government in which our state governments share power with federal institutions. Our structure of overlapping federal, state, and local governance —our country has more than 87,000 different jurisdictions—provides unique opportunity and challenges for our homeland security efforts. The opportunity comes from the expertise and commitment of local agencies and organizations involved in homeland security. The challenge is to develop interconnected and complementary systems that are reinforcing rather than duplicative and that ensure essential requirements are met. A national strategy requires a national effort.

Executive Summary

State and local governments have critical roles to play in homeland security. Indeed, the closest relationship the average citizen has with government is at the local level. State and local levels of government have primary responsibility for funding, preparing, and operating the emergency services that would respond in the event of a terrorist attack. Local units are the first to respond, and the last to leave the scene. All disasters are ultimately local events. The private sector—the Nation's principal provider of goods and services and owner of 85 percent of our infrastructure—is a key homeland security partner. It has a wealth of information that is important to the task of protecting the United States from terrorism. Its creative genius will develop the information systems, vaccines, detection devices, and other technologies and innovations that will secure our homeland. An informed and proactive citizenry is an invaluable asset for our country in times of war and peace.

Volunteers enhance community coordination and action, whether at the national or local level. This coordination will prove critical as we work to build the communication and delivery systems indispensable to our national effort to detect, prevent, and, if need be, respond to terrorist attack.

Critical Mission Areas

The *National Strategy for Homeland Security* aligns and focuses homeland security functions into six critical mission areas: intelligence and warning, border and transportation security, domestic counterterrorism, protecting critical infrastructure, defending against catastrophic terrorism, and emergency preparedness and response. The first three mission areas focus primarily on preventing terrorist attacks; the next two on reducing our Nation's vulnerabilities; and the final one on minimizing the damage and recovering from attacks that do occur. The *Strategy* provides a framework to align the resources of the federal budget directly to the task of securing the homeland. ***Intelligence and Warning.*** Terrorism depends on surprise.With it, a terrorist attack has the potential to do massive damage to an unwitting and unprepared target.Without it, the terrorists stand a good chance of being preempted by authorities, and even if they are not, the damage that results from their attacks is likely to be less severe. The United States will take every necessary action to avoid being surprised by another terrorist attack.We must have an intelligence and warning system that can detect terrorist activity before it manifests itself in an attack so that proper preemptive, preventive, and protective action can be taken.

The *National Strategy for Homeland Security* identifies five major initiatives in this area:

• Enhance the analytic capabilities of the FBI;

• Build new capabilities through the Information Analysis and Infrastructure Protection Division of the proposed Department of Homeland Security;

• Implement the Homeland Security Advisory System;

• Utilize dual-use analysis to prevent attacks; and

• Employ "red team" techniques.

Border and Transportation Security. America historically has relied heavily on two vast oceans and two friendly neighbors for border security, and on the private sector for most forms of domestic transportation security. The increasing mobility and destructive potential of modern terrorism has required the United States to rethink and renovate fundamentally its systems for border and transportation security. Indeed, we must now begin to conceive of border security and transportation security as fully integrated requirements because our domestic transportation systems are inextricably intertwined with the global transport infrastructure. Virtually every community in America is connected to the global transportation network by the seaports, airports, highways, pipelines, railroads, and waterways that move people and goods into, within, and out of the Nation.We must therefore promote the efficient and reliable flow of people, goods, and services across borders, while preventing terrorists from using transportation conveyances or systems to deliver implements of destruction.

The *National Strategy for Homeland Security* identifies six major initiatives in this area: • Ensure accountability in border and transportation security;

- Create "smart borders";

- Increase the security of international shipping containers;

- Implement the Aviation and Transportation Security Act of 2001;

- Recapitalize the U.S. Coast Guard; and

- Reform immigration services.

The President proposed to Congress that the principal border and transportation security agencies—the Immigration and Naturalization Service, the U.S. Customs Service, the U.S. Coast Guard, the Animal and Plant Health Inspection Service, and the

Transportation Security Agency—be transferred to the new Department of Homeland Security. This organizational reform will greatly assist in the implementation of all the above initiatives. ***Domestic Counterterrorism.*** The attacks of September 11 and the catastrophic loss of life and property that resulted have redefined the mission of federal, state, and local law enforcement authorities. While law enforcement agencies will continue to investigate and prosecute criminal activity, they should now assign priority to preventing and interdicting terrorist activity within the United States. The Nation's state and local law enforcement officers will be critical in this effort. Our Nation will use all legal means—both traditional and nontraditional—to identify, halt, and, where appropriate, prosecute terrorists in the United States. We will pursue not only the individuals directly involved in terrorist activity but also their sources of support: the people and organizations that knowingly fund the terrorists and those that provide them with logistical assistance.

Effectively reorienting law enforcement organizations to focus on counterterrorism objectives requires decisive action in a number of areas. The *National Strategy for Homeland Security* identifies six major initiatives in this area:

- Improve intergovernmental law enforcement coordination;

- Facilitate apprehension of potential terrorists;

- Continue ongoing investigations and prosecutions;

• Complete FBI restructuring to emphasize prevention of terrorist attacks;

• Target and attack terrorist financing; and

• Track foreign terrorists and bring them to justice.

Protecting Critical Infrastructure and Key Assets. Our society and modern way of life are dependent on networks of infrastructure—both physical networks such as our energy and transportation systems and virtual networks such as the Internet. If terrorists attack one or more pieces of our critical infrastructure, they may disrupt entire systems and cause significant damage to the Nation. We must therefore improve protection of the individual pieces and interconnecting systems that make up our critical infrastructure. Protecting America's critical infrastructure and key assets will not only make us more secure from terrorist attack, but will also reduce our vulnerability to natural disasters, organized crime, and computer hackers. America's critical infrastructure encompasses a large number of sectors. The U.S. government will seek to deny terrorists the opportunity to inflict lasting harm to our Nation by protecting the assets, systems, and functions vital to our national security, governance, public health and safety, economy, and national morale. The *National Strategy for Homeland Security* identifies eight major initiatives in this area:

• Unify America's infrastructure protection effort in the Department of Homeland Security;

• Build and maintain a complete and accurate assessment of America's critical infrastructure and key assets;

• Enable effective partnership with state and local governments and the private sector;

• Develop a national infrastructure protection plan;

• Secure cyberspace;

• Harness the best analytic and modeling tools to develop effective protective solutions;

• Guard America's critical infrastructure and key assets against "inside" threats; and

• Partner with the international community to protect our transnational infrastructure.

Defending against Catastrophic Threats. The expertise, technology, and material needed to build the most deadly weapons known to mankind—including chemical, biological, radiological, and nuclear weapons —are spreading inexorably. If our enemies acquire these weapons, they are likely to try to use them. The consequences of such an attack could be far more devastating than those we suffered on September 11— a chemical, biological, radiological, or nuclear terrorist attack in the United States could cause large numbers of casualties, mass psychological disruption, contamination and significant economic damage, and could overwhelm local medical capabilities.

Currently, chemical, biological, radiological, and nuclear detection capabilities are modest and response capabilities are dispersed throughout the country at every level of government.While current arrangements have proven adequate for a variety of natural disasters and even the September 11 attacks, the threat of terrorist attacks using chemical, biological, radiological, and nuclear weapons requires new approaches, a focused strategy, and a new organization. The *National Strategy for Homeland Security* identifies six major initiatives in this area:

• Prevent terrorist use of nuclear weapons through better sensors and procedures;

• Detect chemical and biological materials and attacks;

• Improve chemical sensors and decontamination techniques;

• Develop broad spectrum vaccines, antimicrobials, and antidotes;

• Harness the scientific knowledge and tools to counter terrorism;

• Implement the Select Agent Program.

Emergency Preparedness and Response.We must prepare to minimize the damage and recover from any future terrorist attacks that may occur despite our best efforts at prevention. An effective response to a major terrorist incident—as well as a natural disaster—depends on being prepared. Therefore, we need a comprehensive national system to bring together and coordinate all necessary response assets quickly and effectively.We must plan, equip, train, and exercise many different response units to mobilize without warning for any emergency.

Many pieces of this national emergency response system are

already in place. America's first line of defense in the aftermath of any terrorist attack is its first responder community—police officers, fire-fighters, emergency medical providers, public works personnel, and emergency management officials. Nearly three million state and local first responders regularly put their lives on the line to save the lives of others and make our country safer.

Yet multiple plans currently govern the federal government's sup-port of first responders during an incident of national significance. These plans and the government's overarching policy for counterterror-ism are based on an artificial and unnecessary distinction between "cri-sis management" and "consequence management." Under the President's proposal, the Department of Homeland Security will consol-idate federal response plans and build a national system for incident management in cooperation with state and local government. Our feder-al, state, and local governments would ensure that all response person-nel and organizations are properly equipped, trained, and exercised to respond to all terrorist threats and attacks in the United States. Our emergency preparedness and response efforts would also engage the pri-vate sector and the American people.

The *National Strategy for Homeland Security* identifies twelve major initiatives in this area:

• Integrate separate federal response plans into a single all-disci-pline incident management plan;

• Create a national incident management system;

• Improve tactical counterterrorist capabilities;

• Enable seamless communication among all responders;

• Prepare health care providers for catastrophic terrorism;

• Augment America's pharmaceutical and vaccine stockpiles;

• Prepare for chemical, biological, radiological, and nuclear decon-tamination;

• Plan for military support to civil authorities;

• Build the Citizen Corps;

• Implement the First Responder Initiative of the Fiscal Year 2003

Budget;

- Build a national training and evaluation system; and

- Enhance the victim support system.

The Foundations of Homeland Security

The *National Strategy for Homeland Security* also describes four foundations—unique American strengths that cut across all of the mission areas, across all levels of government, and across all sectors of our society. These foundations—law, science and technology, information sharing and systems, and international cooperation—provide a useful framework for evaluating our homeland security investments across the federal government.

Law. Throughout our Nation's history, we have used laws to promote and safeguard our security and our liberty. The law will both provide mechanisms for the government to act and will define the appropriate limits of action.

The *National Strategy for Homeland Security* outlines legislative actions that would help enable our country to fight the war on terrorism more effectively. New federal laws should not preempt state law unnecessarily or overly federalize the war on terrorism. We should guard scrupulously against incursions on our freedoms. The *Strategy* identifies twelve major initiatives in this area:

Federal level

- Enable critical infrastructure information sharing;

- Streamline information sharing among intelligence and law enforcement agencies;

- Expand existing extradition authorities;

- Review authority for military assistance in domestic security;

- Revive the President's reorganization authority; and

- Provide substantial management flexibility for the Department of Homeland Security.

State level

• Coordinate suggested minimum standards for state driver's licenses;

• Enhance market capacity for terrorism insurance;

• Train for prevention of cyber attacks;

• Suppress money laundering;

• Ensure continuity of the judiciary; and

• Review quarantine authorities.

Science and Technology. The Nation's advantage in science and technology is a key to securing the homeland. New technologies for analysis, information sharing, detection of attacks, and countering chemical, biological, radiological, and nuclear weapons will help prevent and minimize the damage from future terrorist attacks. Just as science has helped us defeat past enemies overseas, so too will it help us defeat the efforts of terrorists to attack our homeland and disrupt our way of life.

The federal government is launching a systematic national effort to harness science and technology in support of homeland security. We will build a national research and development enterprise for homeland security sufficient to mitigate the risk posed by modern terrorism. The federal government will consolidate most federally funded homeland security research and development under the Department of Homeland Security to ensure strategic direction and avoid duplicative efforts. We will create and implement a long-term research and development plan that includes investment in revolutionary capabilities with high payoff potential. The federal government will also seek to harness the energy and ingenuity of the private sector to develop and produce the devices and systems needed for homeland security.

The *National Strategy for Homeland Security* identifies eleven major initiatives in this area:

• Develop chemical, biological, radiological, and nuclear countermeasures;

• Develop systems for detecting hostile intent;

• Apply biometric technology to identification devices;

• Improve the technical capabilities of first responders;

• Coordinate research and development of the homeland security apparatus;

• Establish a national laboratory for homeland security;

• Solicit independent and private analysis for science and technology research;

• Establish a mechanism for rapidly producing prototypes;

• Conduct demonstrations and pilot deployments;

• Set standards for homeland security technology; and

• Establish a system for high-risk, high-payoff homeland security research.

Information Sharing and Systems. Information systems contribute to every aspect of homeland security. Although American information technology is the most advanced in the world, our country's information systems have not adequately supported the homeland security mission. Databases used for federal law enforcement, immigration, intelligence, public health surveillance, and emergency management have not been connected in ways that allow us to comprehend where information gaps or redundancies exist. In addition, there are deficiencies in the communications systems used by states and municipalities throughout the country; most state and local first responders do not use compatible communications equipment. To secure the homeland better, we must link the vast amounts of knowledge residing within each government agency while ensuring adequate privacy.

The *National Strategy for Homeland Security* identifies five major initiatives in this area:

• Integrate information sharing across the federal government;

• Integrate information sharing across state and local governments, private industry, and citizens;

• Adopt common "meta-data" standards for electronic information relevant to homeland security;

• Improve public safety emergency communications; and

• Ensure reliable public health information.

International Cooperation. In a world where the terrorist threat pays no respect to traditional bound- THE NATIONAL STRATEGY FOR HOMELAND SECURITY xi aries, our strategy for homeland security cannot stop at our borders. America must pursue a sustained, steadfast, and systematic international agenda to counter the global terrorist threat and improve our homeland security. Our international antiterrorism campaign has made significant progress since September 11. The full scope of these activities will be further described in the forthcoming *National Security Strategy of the United States* and the *National Strategy for Combating Terrorism*. The *National Strategy for Homeland Security* identifies nine major initiatives in this area:

• Create "smart borders";

• Combat fraudulent travel documents;

• Increase the security of international shipping containers;

• Intensify international law enforcement cooperation;

• Help foreign nations fight terrorism;

• Expand protection of transnational critical infrastructure;

• Amplify international cooperation on homeland security science and technology;

• Improve cooperation in response to attacks; and

• Review obligations to international treaties and law.

Costs of Homeland Security

The national effort to enhance homeland security will yield tremendous benefits and entail substantial financial and other costs. Benefits include reductions in the risk of attack and their potential consequences. Costs include not only the resources we commit to homeland security but also the delays to commerce and travel. The United States spends roughly $100 billion per year on homeland security. This figure includes federal, state, and local law enforcement and emergency services, but excludes most funding for the armed forces.

The responsibility of providing homeland security is shared between federal, state and local governments, and the private sector. In many cases, sufficient incentives exist in the private market to supply protection. Government should fund only those homeland security activities that are not supplied, or are inadequately supplied, in the market. Cost sharing between different levels of government should reflect the principles of federalism.Many homeland security activities, such as intelligence gathering and border security, are properly accomplished at the federal level. In other circumstances, such as with first responder capabilities, it is more appropriate for state and local governments to handle these responsibilities.

Conclusion: Priorities for the Future

The *National Strategy for Homeland Security* sets a broad and complex agenda for the United States. The *Strategy* has defined many different goals that need to be met, programs that need to be implemented, and responsibilities that need to be fulfilled. But creating a strategy is, in many respects, about setting priorities— about recognizing that some actions are more critical or more urgent than others.

The President's Fiscal Year 2003 Budget proposal, released in February 2002, identified four priority areas for additional resources and attention in the upcoming year:

- Support first responders;

- Defend against bioterrorism;

- Secure America's borders; and

- Use 21st-century technology to secure the homeland.

Work has already begun on the President's Fiscal Year 2004 Budget. Assuming the Congress passes legislation to implement the President's proposal to create the Department of Homeland Security, the Fiscal Year 2004 Budget will fully reflect the reformed organization of the executive branch for homeland security. That budget will have an integrated and simplified structure based on the six critical mission areas defined by the *Strategy*. Furthermore, at the time the *National Strategy for Homeland Security* was published, it was expected that the Fiscal Year 2004 Budget would attach priority to the following specific items for substantial support:

• Enhance the analytic capabilities of the FBI;

• Build new capabilities through the Information Analysis and Infrastructure Protection Division of the proposed Department of Homeland Security;

• Create "smart borders";

• Improve the security of international shipping containers;

• Recapitalize the U.S. Coast Guard;

• Prevent terrorist use of nuclear weapons through better sensors and procedures;

• Develop broad spectrum vaccines, antimicrobials, and antidotes; and

• Integrate information sharing across the federal government. In the intervening months, the executive branch will prepare detailed implementation plans for these and many other initiatives contained within the *National Strategy for Homeland Security*. These plans will ensure that the taxpayers' money is spent only in a manner that achieves specific objectives with clear performance-based measures of effectiveness. ——————

1 The *National Strategy for Homeland Security* defines "State" to mean "any state of the United States, the District of Columbia, Puerto Rico, the Virgin Islands, Guam, American Samoa, the Canal Zone, the Commonwealth of the Northern Mariana Islands, or the trust territory of the Pacific Islands." The *Strategy* defines "local government" as "any county, city, village, town, district, or other political subdivision of any state, any Native American tribe or authorized tribal organization, or Alaska native village or organization, and includes any rural community or unincorporated town or village or any other public entity for which an application for assistance is made by a state or political subdivision thereof."

2 The distribution of the *National Strategy for Homeland Security* coincides with Congress' consideration of the President's proposal to establish a Department of Homeland Security. The *Strategy* refers to a "Department of Homeland Security" only to provide the strategic vision for the proposed Department and not to assume any one part of the President's proposal will or will not be signed into law.

Our Nation learned a terrible lesson on September 11. American soil is not immune to evil or cold-blooded enemies capable of mass murder and terror. The worst of these enemies—and target number one in our war on terrorism—is the terrorist network Al-Qaeda. Yet the threat to America is not limited to Al-Qaeda or to suicide hijackings of commercial aircraft. The threat is much broader, as we learned on October 4, 2001, when we discovered that a life-threatening biological agent— anthrax—was being distributed through the U.S. mail.

Unless we act to prevent it, a new wave of terrorism, potentially involving the world's most destructive weapons, looms in America's future. It is a challenge as formidable as any ever faced by our Nation. But we are not daunted. We possess the determination and the resources to defeat our enemies and secure our homeland against the threats they pose. Today's terrorists can strike at any place, at any time, and with virtually any weapon. Securing the American homeland is a challenge of monumental scale and complexity. But the U.S. government has no more important mission.

CHAPTER 2
National Strategy for Homeland Security

This document is the first ever *National Strategy for Homeland Security*. The purpose of the *Strategy* is to mobilize and organize our Nation to secure the U.S. homeland from terrorist attacks. This is an exceedingly complex mission that requires coordinated and focused effort from our entire society—the federal government, state and local governments, the private sector, and the American people.

People and organizations all across the United States have taken many steps to improve our security since the September 11 attacks, but a great deal of work remains. The *National Strategy for Homeland Security* will help prepare our Nation for the work ahead in several ways. It provides direction to the federal government departments and agencies that have a role in homeland security. It suggests steps that state and local governments, private companies and organizations, and individual Americans can take to improve our security, and offers incentives for them to do so. It recommends certain actions to the Congress. In this way, the *Strategy* provides a framework for the contributions that we all can make to secure our homeland. The *National Strategy for Homeland Security* is the beginning of what will be a long struggle to protect our Nation from terrorism. It provides a foundation upon which to organize our efforts and provides initial guidance to prioritize the work ahead. The *Strategy* will be adjusted and amended over time. We must be prepared to adapt as our enemies in the war on terrorism adjust their means of attack.

Homeland Security Defined

In the aftermath of September 11, "homeland security" has come to mean many things to many people. It is a new mission and a new term. The federal government defines homeland security as follows: Each phrase in the definition has meaning.

Concerted national effort. The federal government has a critical role to play in homeland security. Yet the nature of American society and the structure of American governance make it impossible to achieve the goal of a secure homeland through federal executive branch action alone. The Administration's approach to homeland security is based on the principles of shared responsibility and partnership with the Congress, state and local governments, the private sector, and the American people. The *National Strategy for Homeland Security* belongs and applies to the Nation as a whole, not just to the President's proposed Department of Homeland Security or the federal government.

Prevent. The first priority of homeland security is to prevent terrorist attacks. The United States aims to deter all potential terrorists from attacking America through our uncompromising commitment to defeating terrorism wherever it appears. We also strive to detect terrorists before they strike, to prevent them and their instruments of terror from entering our country, and to take decisive action to eliminate the threat they pose. These efforts—which will be described in both the *National Strategy for Homeland Security* and the *National Strategy for Combating Terrorism*—take place both at home and abroad. The nature of modern terrorism requires a global approach to prevention.

The *National Strategy for Homeland Security* attaches special emphasis to preventing, protecting against, and preparing for catastrophic threats. The greatest risk of mass casualties, massive property loss, and immense social disruption comes from weapons of mass destruction, strategic information warfare, attacks on critical infrastructure, and attacks on the highest leadership of government.

Terrorist attacks. Homeland security is focused on terrorism in the United States. The *National Strategy for Homeland Security* characterizes terrorism as any premeditated, unlawful act dangerous to human life or public welfare that is intended to intimidate or coerce civilian populations or governments. This description captures the core concepts shared by the various definitions of terrorism contained in the U.S. Code, each crafted to achieve a legal standard of specificity and clarity. This description covers kidnappings; hijackings; shootings; conventional bombings; attacks involving chemical, biological, radiological, or nuclear weapons; cyber attacks; and any number of other forms of malicious violence. Terrorists can be U.S. citizens or foreigners, acting in concert with others, on their own, or on behalf of a hostile state.

Reduce America's vulnerability. Homeland security involves a systematic, comprehensive, and strategic effort to reduce America's vulnerability to terrorist attack. We must recognize that as a vibrant and prosperous free society, we present an ever-evolving, ever-changing target. As we shore up our defenses in one area, the terrorists may exploit vulnerabilities in others. The *National Strategy for Homeland Security*, therefore, outlines a way for the government to work with the private sector to identify and protect our critical infrastructure and key assets, detect terrorist threats, and augment our defenses.

Because we must not permit the threat of terrorism to alter the American way of life, we have to accept some level of terrorist risk as a permanent condition. We must constantly balance the benefits of mitigating this risk against both the economic costs and infringements on individual liberty that this mitigation entails. No mathematical formula can reveal the appropriate balance; it must be determined by politically accountable leaders exercising sound, considered judgment informed by top-notch scientists, medical experts, and engineers.

Definition

Homeland security is a concerted national effort to prevent terrorist attacks within the United States, reduce America's vulnerability to terrorism, and minimize the damage and recover from attacks that do occur.

Minimize the damage. The United States will prepare to manage the consequences of any future terrorist attacks that may occur despite our best efforts at prevention. Therefore, homeland security seeks to improve the systems and prepare the individuals that will respond to acts of terror. The *National Strategy for Homeland Security* recognizes that after an attack occurs, our greatest chance to minimize loss of life and property lies with our local first responders—police officers, firefighters, emergency medical providers, public works personnel, and emergency management officials. Many of our efforts to minimize the damage focus on these brave and dedicated public servants.

Recover. As an essential component of homeland security, the United States will build and maintain various financial, legal, and social systems to recover from all forms of terrorism. We must, therefore, be prepared to protect and restore institutions needed to sustain economic growth and confidence, rebuild destroyed property, assist victims and their families, heal psychological wounds, and demonstrate compassion, recognizing that we cannot automatically return to the pre-attack norm.

Principles of the *National Strategy for Homeland Security*

Our efforts in the war on terrorism are rooted in the same core American strengths and characteristics that led us to victory in World War II and the Cold War: innovation, determination, and commitment to the democratic tenets of freedom and equality.With these strengths and characteristics as our guide, eight principles have shaped the design of the *National Strategy for Homeland Security.*

Require responsibility and accountability. The *National Strategy for Homeland Security* is focused on producing results.When possible, it designates lead executive branch departments or agencies for federal homeland security initiatives. As the President announced on June 6, 2002, the *Strategy* calls for creating the Department of Homeland Security to clarify lines of responsibility for homeland security in the executive branch. The new Department would take responsibility for many of the initiatives outlined here. The *Strategy* also makes recommendations to Congress, state and local governments, the private sector, and the American people.

Mobilize our entire society. The *National Strategy for Homeland Security* recognizes the crucial role of state and local governments, private institutions, and the American people in securing our homeland. Our traditions of federalism and limited government require that organizations outside the federal government take the lead in many of these efforts. The *Strategy* provides guidance on best practices and organizing principles. It also seeks to empower all key players by streamlining and clarifying federal support processes.

Manage risk and allocate resources judiciously. The *National Strategy for Homeland Security* identifies priority programs for our finite homeland security resources. Because the number of potential terrorist acts is nearly infinite, we must make difficult choices about how to allocate resources against those risks that pose the greatest danger to our homeland. The concluding chapter of the *Strategy* identifies a set of priorities for the Fiscal Year 2004 Federal Budget.

Seek opportunity out of adversity. The *National Strategy for Homeland Security* gives special attention to programs that improve security while at the same time advancing other important public purposes or principles.We will build, for example, a national incident management system that is better able to manage not just terrorism but other hazards such as natural disasters and industrial accidents. We will build a medical system that is not simply better able to cope with bioterrorism but with all diseases and all manner of mass-casualty incidents. We will build a border

Objectives of the *National Strategy for Homeland Security*

Homeland security is an exceedingly complex mission. It involves efforts both at home and abroad. It demands a range of government and private sector capabilities. And it calls for coordinated and focused effort from many actors who are not otherwise required to work together and for whom security is not always a primary mission. This *Strategy* establishes three objectives based on the definition of homeland security:

• Prevent terrorist attacks within the United States;

• Reduce America's vulnerability to terrorism; and

• Minimize the damage and recover from attacks that do occur. The order of these objectives deliberately sets priorities for America's efforts to secure the homeland. management system that will not only stop terrorist penetration but will also facilitate the efficient flow of legitimate commerce and people.

Foster flexibility. The *National Strategy for Homeland Security* emphasizes the need for a flexible response to terrorism. The terrorist threat is ever-changing because our terrorist enemies can strategically adapt their offensive tactics to exploit what they perceive to be weaknesses in our defenses. Therefore, the *Strategy* builds managerial, budgetary, and structural flexibility into the federal government's homeland security structure and suggests similar measures for the rest of the Nation. It allows for the reassessment of priorities and the realignment of resources as the terrorist threat evolves.

Measure preparedness. The *National Strategy for Homeland Security* demands accountability from every government body responsible for homeland security initiatives. Every department or agency will create benchmarks and other performance measures by which we can evaluate our progress and allocate future resources.

Sustain efforts over the long term. Protecting the homeland from terrorist attack is a permanent mission. Therefore, the *National Strategy for Homeland Security* provides an initial set of initiatives for moving closer to our homeland security objectives. Lead departments and agencies should plan to sustain homeland security initiatives for years and decades, not weeks and months.

Constrain government spending. The *National Strategy for Homeland Security* does not equate more money spent to more security earned. So in addition to new or expanded federal programs, the *Strategy* also calls for government reorganization, legal reform, essential regulation, incentives, cost-sharing arrangements with state and local governments, cooperative arrangements with the private sector, and the organized involvement of citizens. The *Strategy* recognizes that the capabilities and laws we rely upon to defend America against terrorism are closely linked to those which we rely upon to deal with non-terrorist phenomena such as crime, natural disease, natural disasters, and national security incidents. The *Strategy* aims to build upon and improve the coordination of these existing systems. It also seeks to harness the extraordinary strength and creativity of the private sector by allowing the market to solve homeland security shortfalls whenever possible.

Implementing the *National Strategy for Homeland Security*

The *National Strategy for Homeland Security* establishes, for the first time in our Nation's history, a statement of objectives around which our entire society can mobilize to secure the U.S. homeland from the dangerous and evolving threat of terrorism.

The *National Strategy for Homeland Security* aligns and focuses homeland security functions into six critical mission areas: intelligence and warning, border and transportation security, domestic counterterrorism, protecting critical infrastructure and key assets, defending against catastrophic terrorism, and emergency preparedness and response. The first three mission areas focus primarily on preventing terrorist attacks; the next two on reducing our Nation's vulnerabilities; and the final one on minimizing the damage and recovering from attacks that do occur. The *Strategy* includes the President's proposal to establish, for the first time, clear responsibility and accountability for each of these critical mission areas—most importantly, a Secretary of Homeland Security who is appointed by the President and confirmed by the Senate. The *National Strategy for Homeland Security* provides, for the first time, a framework to align the resources of the federal budget directly to the task of securing the homeland. Every homeland security dollar in the President's Budget for Fiscal Year 2004 will correspond with the strategy's critical mission areas. The *Strategy* also describes four foundations—unique American strengths that cut across all of the mission areas, across all levels of government, and across all sectors of our society. These foundations—law, science and technology, information sharing and systems, and international cooperation—provide a useful framework for evaluating our homeland security investments across the federal government.

The *National Strategy for Homeland Security* is, however, only a first step in a long-term effort to secure the homeland. The federal executive branch will use a variety of tools to implement the *Strategy*. The Administration will work with Congress to craft future federal homeland security budgets based on the *Strategy*, providing every department and agency involved in homeland security the required resources to execute its responsibilities. Each lead department and agency will plan and program to execute the initiatives assigned by the *National Strategy for Homeland Security*. Each department and agency will also be accountable for its performance on homeland security efforts. The federal government will employ performance measures—and encourage the same for state and local governments—to evaluate the effectiveness of each homeland security program. These performance measures will allow agencies to measure their progress, make resource allocation decisions, and adjust priorities accordingly.

Under the President's proposal, the Department of Homeland Security will play a central role in implementing the *National Strategy for Homeland Security*. In addition to executing its assigned initiatives, the Department would also serve as the primary federal point of contact for state and local governments, the private sector, and the American people. Working with the White House, the Department therefore would coordinate and support implementation of non-federal tasks recommended in the *Strategy*. Issuance of the *Strategy* overlaps with Congress' consideration of the President's proposal to establish the Department. Recognizing that Congress alone can create a new Department, references to a "Department of Homeland Security" are intended only to provide the strategic vision for the proposed Department.

The Preamble to the Constitution defines our federal government's basic purposes as "… to form a more perfect Union, establish justice, insure domestic Tranquility, provide for the common defense, promote the general Welfare, and secure the Blessings of Liberty to ourselves and our Posterity." The requirement to provide for the common defense remains as fundamental today as it was when these words were written, more than two hundred years ago.

The *National Security Strategy of the United States* aims to guarantee the sovereignty and independence of the United States, with our fundamental values and institutions intact. It provides a framework for creating and seizing opportunities that strengthen our security and prosperity. The *National Strategy for Homeland Security* complements the *National Security Strategy of the United States* by addressing a very specific and uniquely challenging threat – terrorism in the United States – and by providing a comprehensive framework for organizing the efforts of federal, state, local and private organizations whose primary functions are often unrelated to national security.

The link between national security and homeland security is a subtle but important one. For more than six decades, America has sought to protect its own sovereignty and independence through a strategy of global presence and engagement. In so doing, America has helped many other countries and peoples advance along the path of democracy, open markets, individual liberty, and peace with their neighbors. Yet there are those who oppose America's role in the world, and who are willing to use violence against us and our friends. Our great power leaves these enemies with few conventional options for doing us harm. One such option is to take advantage of our freedom and openness by secretly inserting terrorists into our country to attack our homeland. Homeland security seeks to deny this avenue of attack to our enemies and thus to provide a secure foundation for America's ongoing global engagement. Thus the *National Security Strategy of the United States* and *National Strategy for Homeland Security* work as mutually supporting documents, providing guidance to the executive branch departments and agencies.

There are also a number of other, more specific strategies maintained by the United States that are subsumed within the twin concepts of national security and homeland security. The *National Strategy for Combating Terrorism* will define the U.S. war plan against international terrorism. The *National Strategy to Combat Weapons of Mass Destruction* coordinates America's many efforts to deny terrorists and states the materials, technology, and expertise to make and deliver weapons of mass destruction. The *National Strategy to Secure Cyberspace* will describe our initiatives to secure our information systems against deliberate, malicious disruption. The *National Money Laundering Strategy* aims to undercut the illegal flows of money that support terrorism and international criminal activity. The *National Defense Strategy* sets priorities for our most powerful national security instrument. The *National Drug Control Strategy* lays out a comprehensive U.S. effort to combat drug smuggling and consumption. All of these documents fit into the framework established by the *National Security Strategy of the United States* and *National Strategy for Homeland Security,* which together take precedence over all other national strategies, programs, and plans.

The U.S. government has no higher purpose than to ensure the security of our people and preserve our democratic way of life. Terrorism directly threatens the foundations of our Nation—our people, our democratic way of life, and our economic prosperity. In the war on terrorism, as in all wars, the more we know about our enemy, the better able we are to defeat that enemy. The more we know about our vulnerability, the better able we are to protect ourselves.

One fact dominates all homeland security threat assessments: terrorists are strategic actors. They choose their targets deliberately based on the weaknesses they observe in our defenses and our preparations. They can balance the difficulty in successfully executing a particular attack against the magnitude of loss it might cause. They can monitor our media and listen to our policymakers as our Nation discusses how to protect itself—and adjust their plans accordingly. Where we insulate ourselves from one form of attack, they can shift and focus on another exposed vulnerability. We remain a Nation at war. Even as we experience success in the war on terrorism, the antipathy of our enemies may well be increasing, and new enemies may emerge. The United States will confront the threat of terrorism for the foreseeable future.

CHAPTER 3
Threat and Vulnerability

Our Free Society Is Inherently Vulnerable

The American people and way of life are the primary targets of our enemy, and our highest protective priority. Our population and way of life are the source of our Nation's great strength, but also a source of inherent vulnerability. Our population is large, diverse, and highly mobile, allowing terrorists to hide within our midst. Americans congregate at schools, sporting arenas, malls, concert halls, office buildings, high-rise residences, and places of worship, presenting targets with the potential for many casualties. Much of America lives in densely populated urban areas, making our major cities conspicuous targets. Americans subsist on the produce of farms in rural areas nationwide, making our heartland a potential target for agroterrorism. The responsibility of our government extends beyond the physical well-being of the American people. We must also safeguard our way of life, which involves five key elements: democracy, liberties, security, economics, and culture.

Democracy. Our way of life is both defined and protected by our democratic political system. It is a system anchored by the Constitution, which established a republic characterized by significant limits on governmental power through a system of checks and balances, a distribution of state and federal rights, and an affirmation of the rights and freedoms of individuals. Our democratic political system is transparent and accessible to the populace. It requires that all actions adhere to the rule of law. And it relies on the stability and continuity of our government, which is ensured by constitutionally prescribed procedures and powers.

Liberties. Liberty and freedom are fundamental to our way of life. Freedom of expression, freedom of religion, freedom of movement, property rights, freedom from unlawful discrimination—these are all rights we are guaranteed as Americans, and rights we will fight to protect. Many have fought and died in order to establish and protect these rights; we will not relinquish them.

Security. Our federal system was born, in part, out of a need to "provide for the common defense." Americans have enjoyed great security from external threats, with no hostile powers adjacent to our borders and insulated from attack by two vast oceans. Our approach to security has had both external and internal dimensions. Externally, the United States has over the course of the past six decades sought to shape the international environment through strong global political, economic, military, and cultural engagement. Internally, we have relied primarily on law enforcement and the justice system to provide for domestic peace and order.

Economy. Our country's economy is based on a free market system predicated on private ownership of property and freedom of contract, with limited government intervention.We ask our able population to work for their individual prosperity, as our government ensures that all have equal access to the marketplace. Our formula for prosperity is one that has succeeded: we are the most prosperous Nation in the world.

Culture. The United States of America is an open, welcoming, pluralistic, diverse society that engages in dialogue rather than the dogmatic enforcement of any one set of values or ideas. Our culture is also characterized by compassion and strong civic engagement.

The American Population

• An estimated 284.8 million people lived in the United States on July 1, 2001 *Source: U.S. Department of Commerce*

• 54.2% of the Nation's population lives in ten states – three in the Northeast, three in the Midwest, three in the South, and one in the West

• The average population density within the United States is 79.2 people per square mile of land

• The average population density in metropolitan areas is 320.2 people per square mile of land

• Over 225 million Americans live in metropolitan areas

• Nearly 85 million Americans live in metropolitan areas of 5 million people or more

• Each year, the United States admits 500 million people, including

330 million noncitizens, through our borders

Source: 2000 Census

• Over 4 million people were processed through security at the last Olympics, over 85,000 at the last Super Bowl, and approximately 20,000 each at the Republican and Democratic National Conventions.

Source: U.S. Secret Service

The Means of Attack

Terrorism is not so much a system of belief, like fascism or communism, as it is a strategy and a tactic— a means of attack. In this war on terrorism, we must defend ourselves against a wide range of means and methods of attack. Our enemies are working to obtain chemical, biological, radiological, and nuclear weapons for the stated purpose of killing vast numbers of Americans. Terrorists continue to employ conventional means of attack, such as bombs and guns. At the same time, they are gaining expertise in less traditional means, such as cyber attacks. Lastly, as we saw on September 11, our terrorist enemies are constantly seeking new tactics or unexpected ways to carry out their attacks and magnify their effects.

Weapons of mass destruction. The knowledge, technology, and materials needed to build weapons of mass destruction are spreading. These capabilities have never been more accessible and the trends are not in our favor. If our terrorist enemies acquire these weapons and the means to deliver them, they are likely to try to use them, with potential consequences far more devastating than those we suffered on September 11. Terrorists may conceivably steal or obtain weapons of mass destruction, weapons-usable fissile material, or related technology from states with such capabilities. Several state sponsors of terrorism already possess or are working to develop weapons of mass destruction, and could provide material or technical support to terrorist groups.

Chemical weapons are extremely lethal and capable of producing tens of thousands of casualties. They are also relatively easy to manufacture, using basic equipment, trained personnel, and precursor materials that often have legitimate dual uses. As the 1995 Tokyo subway attack revealed, even sophisticated nerve agents are within the reach of terrorist groups. Biological weapons, which release large quantities of living, disease-causing microorganisms, have extraordinary lethal potential. Like chemical weapons, biological weapons are relatively easy to manufacture, requiring straightforward technical skills, basic equipment, and a seed stock of pathogenic microorganisms. Biological weapons are especially dangerous because we may not know immediately that we have been attacked, allowing an infectious agent time to spread. Moreover, biological agents can serve as a means of attack against humans as well as livestock and crops, inflicting casualties as well as economic damage.

Radiological weapons, or "dirty bombs," combine radioactive material with conventional explosives. They can cause widespread disruption and fear, particularly in heavily populated areas. Nuclear weapons have enormous destructive potential. Terrorists who seek to develop a nuclear weapon must overcome two formidable challenges. First, acquiring or refining a sufficient quantity of fissile material is very difficult—though not impossible. Second, manufacturing a workable weapon requires a very high degree of technical capability— though terrorists could feasibly assemble the simplest type of nuclear device.

To get around these significant though not insurmountable challenges, terrorists could seek to steal or purchase a nuclear weapon.

Conventional means. While we must prepare for attacks that employ the most destructive weapons, we must also defend against the tactics that terrorists employ most frequently. Terrorists, both domestic and international, continue to use traditional methods of violence and destruction to inflict harm and spread fear. They have used knives, guns, and bombs to kill the innocent. They have taken hostages and spread propaganda. Given the low expense, ready availability of materials, and relatively high chance for successful execution, terrorists will continue to make use of conventional attacks.

Cyber attacks. Terrorists may seek to cause widespread disruption and damage, including casualties, by attacking our electronic and computer networks, which are linked to other critical infrastructures such as our energy, financial, and securities networks. Terrorist groups are already exploiting new information technology and the Internet to plan attacks, raise funds, spread propaganda, collect information, and communicate securely. As terrorists further develop their technical capabilities and become more familiar with potential targets, cyber attacks will become an increasingly significant threat.

New or unexpected tactics. Our terrorist enemies are constantly seeking new tactics or unexpected ways to carry out attacks. They are continuously trying to find new areas of vulnerability and apply lessons learned from past operations in order to achieve surprise and maximize the destructive effect of their next attack. Our society presents an almost infinite array of potential targets, allowing for an enormously wide range of potential attack methods.

The Terrorists

Our enemies seek to remain invisible, lurking in the shadows. We are taking aggressive action to uncover individuals and groups engaged in terrorist activity, but often we will not know who our enemy is by name until after they have attempted to attack us. Therefore, we must uncover more than just the identities of our enemy. We need to analyze the characteristics shared by terrorists to help us understand where our enemies are weak and where they are strong.

Terrorists and their tactical advantages. Terrorists enjoy certain tactical advantages. They are able to choose the time, place, and method of their attacks. As we reduce our vulnerabilities in one area, they can alter their plans and pursue more exposed targets. They are able to patiently plan their attacks for months and years. Plans are undoubtedly underway today by terrorist cells that we have not yet eliminated. Terrorists also exploit the advantage of relative anonymity. They hide throughout the world, using the cover of innocent civilians as a shield. Weak states will remain susceptible to terrorist groups seeking safe haven, and may even cooperate with or actively support terrorists.

Known terrorist groups. Al-Qaeda remains America's most immediate and serious threat despite our success in disrupting its network in Afghanistan and elsewhere. While we have captured or killed hundreds of Al-Qaeda operatives, many remain at large, including leaders working to reconstitute the organization and resume its operations. Al-Qaeda operatives and cells will continue to plan attacks against highprofile landmarks and critical infrastructure at home and against targets in Europe, the Middle East, Africa, and Southeast Asia. Those attacks may use both conventional and unconventional means in an effort to create as much destruction and kill as many people as possible.

Al-Qaeda is part of a dangerous trend toward sophisticated terrorist networks spread across many countries, linked together by information technology, enabled by far-flung networks of financial and ideological supporters, and operating in a highly decentralized manner. Unlike traditional adversaries, these terrorist networks have no single "center of gravity" whose destruction would entail the defeat of the entire organization. While we have denied Afghanistan as a safe haven for Al-Qaeda, unrest in politically unstable regions will continue to create an environment conducive to terrorism and capable of providing sanctuary to terrorist groups. Moreover, an unknown number of terrorist cells operate from within Western democracies, where the safeguarding of civil liberties protects them as well as their potential victims.

Al-Qaeda is only part of a broader threat that includes other international terrorist organizations with the will and capability to attack the United States. The most dangerous of these groups are associated with religious extremist movements in the Middle East and South Asia. Until September 11, Hizballah was responsible for more American deaths than all other terrorist groups combined, including those killed in the 1983 bombing of the U.S. Marine Corps barracks in Lebanon. Hizballah has never carried out an attack within the United States, but could do so if the situation in the Middle East worsens or the group feels threatened by U.S. actions. Other terrorist groups, from Hamas to the Real Irish Republican Army, have supporters in the United States. To date, most of these groups have largely limited their activities in the United States to fundraising, recruiting, and low-level intelligence, but many are capable of carrying out terrorist acts within the United States.

Terrorist groups also include domestic organizations. The 1995 bombing of the Murrah Federal Building in Oklahoma City highlights the threat of domestic terrorist acts designed to achieve mass casualties. The U.S. government averted seven planned terrorist acts in 1999— two were potentially large-scale, high-casualty attacks being organized by domestic extremist groups. Both domestic terrorist groups (such as the National Alliance, the Aryan Nation, and the extremist Puerto Rican separatist group Los Macheteros) and special interest extremist groups continue to pose a threat to the peace and stability of our country.

The tactics of modern terrorists are unbounded by the traditional rules of warfare. Terrorists transform objects of daily life into weapons, visiting death and destruction on unsuspecting civilians. Defeating this enemy requires a focused and organized response. The President took a critical step by proposing the creation of the Department of Homeland Security.

CHAPTER 4
Organizing for a Secure Homeland

The creation of the Department, the most significant reorganization of the federal government in more than a half-century, will give the United States a foundation for our efforts to secure the homeland. The Department would serve as the unifying core of the vast national network of organizations and institutions involved in homeland security.

American Federalism and Homeland Security

American democracy is rooted in the precepts of federalism —a system of government in which our state governments share power with federal institutions. The Tenth Amendment reserves to the states and to the people all power not specifically delegated to the federal government. Our structure of overlapping federal, state, and local governance—the United States has more than 87,000 different jurisdictions— provides unique opportunities and challenges. The opportunity comes from the expertise and commitment of local agencies and organizations involved in homeland security. The challenge is to develop complementary systems that avoid duplication and ensure essential requirements are met. To meet the terrorist threat, we must increase collaboration and coordination—in law enforcement and prevention, emergency response and recovery, policy development and implementation—so that public and private resources are better aligned to secure the homeland.

American People

All of us have a key role to play in America's war on terrorism. Terrorists may live and travel among us and attack our homes and our places of business, governance, and recreation. In order to defeat an enemy who uses our very way of life as a weapon—who takes advantage of our freedoms and liberties—every American must be willing to do his or her part to protect our homeland.

Since September 11, thousands of individuals have stepped forward to ask, "What can I do to help?" The President launched Citizen Corps in January 2002 to help channel this volunteerism, and individuals in all 50 states and U.S. territories have signed up since. In support of this effort, Citizen Corps released a guidebook—produced by the National Crime Prevention Council with support from the Department of Justice—to provide the American people with information about the latest disaster preparedness techniques. As part of Citizen Corps, the Federal Emergency Management Agency's Community Emergency Response Team program trains volunteers to support our first responders by providing immediate help to victims and by organizing volunteers at disaster sites. Citizen Corps is expanding the Neighborhood Watch Program to incorporate terrorism prevention and education into its existing crime prevention mission. Volunteers in Police Service will encourage the use of civilian volunteers to support resourceconstrained police departments. The Medical Reserve Corps will provide communities with medical volunteers —both active and retired—who can assist health care professionals during a large-scale local emergency. Finally, Operation TIPS (Terrorism Information and Prevention System) will be a nationwide program to help thousands of American truck drivers, letter carriers, train conductors, ship captains, and utility workers report potential terrorist activity. Operation TIPS will begin a pilot program in ten cities in August 2002.

Private Sector

Given our traditions of limited government, the American private sector provides most of our goods and services. Private companies are a key source of new ideas and innovative technologies that will enable us to triumph over the terrorist threat. There are, for example, pharmaceutical companies producing new vaccines against dangerous biological agents and information technology firms investing in new communications technology for first responders. The President has sought to tap into this creative genius by establishing a national Homeland Security Advisory Council and calling on private citizens to serve on similar boards at the state and local level.

The private sector also owns the vast majority of America's critical infrastructure. It includes crucial systems such as the agricultural and food distribution processes that put food on our tables, utility companies that provide water and power to our homes and businesses, and transportation systems that fly us from city to city and bus our children to and from school. The private sector also includes many of our academic institutions and a host of scientific, medical, engineering, and technological research facilities. A close partnership between the government and private sector is essential to ensuring that existing vulnerabilities to terrorism in our critical infrastructure are identified and eliminated as quickly as possible. The private sector should conduct risk assessments on their holdings and invest in systems to protect key assets. The internalization of these costs is not only a matter of sound corporate governance and good corporate citizenship but also an essential safeguard of economic assets for shareholders, employees, and the Nation. (See *Costs of Homeland Security* chapter for additional discussion.)

State and Local Governments

State, county, municipal, and local governments fund and operate the emergency services that would respond in the event of a terrorist attack. Ultimately, all manmade and natural disasters are local events— with local units being the first to respond and the last to leave. Since September 11, every state and many cities and counties are addressing homeland security issues either through an existing office or through a newly created office. Many have established anti-terrorism task forces. Many have also published or are preparing homeland security strategies, some based on existing plans for dealing with natural disasters. Each level of government must coordinate with other levels to minimize redundancies in homeland security actions and ensure integration of efforts. The federal government must seek to utilize state and local knowledge about their communities and then share relevant information with the state and local entities positioned to act on it. (A summary of homeland security actions taken to date by states, counties, and cities is contained in a companion volume.)

Federal Executive Branch

The President's most important job is to protect the American people. To do so, he relies on the departments and agencies of the executive branch, which are responsible for executing and enforcing the federal laws, as well as the White House and other offices of the Executive Office of the President, which develop and implement his policies and programs.

Department of Homeland Security. The President's proposal to create the Department of Homeland Security is the outcome of a comprehensive study of the federal government's current structure, the experience gained since September 11, and the new information we have learned about our enemies while fighting a war. The new Department would bring together 22 entities with critical homeland security missions and would provide us for the first time with a single federal department whose primary mission is to protect our homeland against terrorist threats. The Department would play a central role in implementing the *National Strategy for Homeland Security.* It would be responsible for many specific initiatives and would also streamline relations with the federal government for our state and local governments, private sector, and the American people. This Department, although focused primarily on homeland security, would continue to execute the non-homeland security missions of its constituent parts.

White House Office of Homeland Security. Even after the Department of Homeland Security begins to function, the White House Office of Homeland Security will continue to play a key role advising the President and coordinating the interagency process. It will continue to work with the Office of Management and Budget to develop and defend the President's homeland security budget proposals. It will certify that the budgets of other executive branch departments will enable them to carry out their homeland security responsibilities.

Department of Defense. The Department of Defense contributes to homeland security through its military missions overseas, homeland defense, and support to civil authorities. Ongoing military operations abroad have reduced the terrorist threat against the United States. There are three circumstances under which the Department would be involved in improving security at home. In extraordinary circumstances, the Department would conduct military missions such as combat air patrols or maritime defense operations.

The Department would take the lead in defending the people and the territory of our country, supported by other agencies. Plans for such contingencies will continue to be coordinated, as appropriate, with the National Security Council, Homeland Security Council, and other federal departments and agencies. Second, the Department of Defense would be involved during emergencies such as responding to an attack or to forest fires, floods, tornadoes, or other catastrophes. In these circumstances, the Department may be asked to act quickly to provide capabilities that other agencies do not have. Finally, the Department of Defense would also take part in "limited scope" missions where other agencies have the lead—for example, security at a special event like the recent Olympics.

Other federal departments and agencies. Many other government departments and agencies support homeland security as part of their overall mission. The Attorney General, as America's chief law enforcement officer, will lead our Nation's law enforcement effort to detect, prevent, and investigate terrorist activity within the United States. The Department of Agriculture's Food Safety Inspection and Agricultural Research Services have important homeland security responsibilities for preventing agroterrorism. The Centers for Disease Control and Prevention and the National Institutes of Health, both part of the Department of Health and Human Services, provide critical expertise and resources related to bioterrorism. Several other federal entities have significant counterterrorism intelligence responsibilities, including the CIA's Counterterrorist Center and the FBI's Counterterrorism Division and Criminal Intelligence Section. The CIA is specifically responsible for gathering and analyzing all information regarding potential terrorist threats abroad. The proposed Information Analysis and Infrastructure Protection Division within the Department of Homeland Security would be able not only to access and analyze homeland security information, but also to translate it into warning and protective action.

Intergovernmental coordination. There is a vital need for cooperation between the federal government and state and local governments on a scale never before seen in the United States. Cooperation must occur both horizontally (within each level of government) and vertically (among various levels of government). Under the President's proposal, the creation of the Department of Homeland Security will simplify the process by which governors, mayors, and county leaders interact with the federal government.We cannot and will not create separate and specialized coordinating bodies for every functional area of government. To do so would merely replicate the stovepiped system that exists today and would defeat a main purpose of creating the new Department.

Because of our federalist traditions and our large number of local governments, the federal government must look to state governments to facilitate close coordination and cooperation among all levels of government—federal, state, and local. Therefore, the President calls on each governor to establish a single Homeland Security Task Force (HSTF) for the state, to serve as his or her primary coordinating body with the federal government. This would realign the existing Anti-Terrorism Task Forces, established after September 11 in 93 federal judicial districts nationwide, to serve as the law enforcement component of the broader HSTFs. The HSTFs would provide a collaborative, cost-effective structure for effectively communicating to all organizations and citizens. They would help streamline and coordinate all federal, regional, and local programs.They would also fit neatly into the regional emergency response network that the Department of Homeland Security would inherit from FEMA.

CHAPTER 5
Intelligence and Warning

Terrorism depends on surprise.With it, a terrorist attack has the potential to do massive damage to an unwitting and unprepared target.Without it, the terrorists stand a good chance of being thwarted by authorities, and even if they are not, the damage from their attacks is likely to be less severe. It follows that the United States must take every appropriate action to avoid being surprised by another terrorist attack. To secure the homeland, we must have an intelligence and warning system that is capable of detecting terrorist activity before it manifests itself in an attack so that proper preemptive, preventive, and protective action can be taken.

This is not the first time in American history that we have had to focus on our early warning capabilities. The Japanese attack on Pearl Harbor on December 7, 1941, demonstrated the catastrophic consequences of allowing an enemy to achieve even tactical surprise. With the dawn of the nuclear age, early warning became essential to national survival. The United States spent billions of dollars during the Cold War on ground- and space-based sensors that had one principal, overriding purpose: to detect indications of a nuclear attack by the Soviet Union. These early warning systems were the foundation for strategic nuclear deterrence because they provided the President sufficient lead-time to make retaliatory decisions.

Early warning of an impending terrorist attack is a far more difficult and complex mission than was early warning of a strategic nuclear
first strike.Whereas we almost always know the identity, location, and
general capabilities of hostile nations, we frequently do not know the
identity or location of non-state terrorist organizations. The indications
of terrorist intent are often ambiguous. Terrorists are able to infiltrate
and move freely within democratic countries making themselves effectively invisible against the backdrop of an enormously diverse and
mobile society. Efforts to gather intelligence on potential terrorist
threats can affect the basic rights and liberties of American citizens.

Moreover, the question of how to achieve early warning of terrorist threats is inseparable from the question of what to do with some
warning information once it is in hand.What preventive action should be
taken? What protective action should be taken? To whom should the
information be provided on a confidential basis? Should the public be
informed and, if so, how and by whom? These very concrete decisions
can have life-or-death implications. Unfortunately, the ambiguous
nature of most intelligence on terrorist threats means that these decisions must often be made in conditions of great uncertainty.

America's intelligence community has made significant contributions to our national security and is now making adjustments to help
meet the increased needs for homeland security. At present, we have
insufficient human source intelligence developed overseas about potential terrorist activities in the United States. Agencies at all levels of government have not always fully shared homeland security information
due to real and perceived legal and cultural barriers, as well as the lim-
itations of their information systems. The United States needs to do a
better job of utilizing information contained in foreign-language documents that we have obtained. In addition, our intelligence community
must identify, collect, and analyze the new observables that will enable
us to better understand emerging unconventional threats.

The *National Strategy for Homeland Security* reflects the concept
that intelligence and information analysis is not a separate, stand-alone
activity but rather an integral component of our Nation's overall effort
to protect against and reduce our vulnerability to terrorism. The basic
roles and responsibilities in this *Strategy* are depicted in Figure 1.

This framework recognizes four interrelated but distinct categories
of intelligence and information analysis, as well as three broad cate-

gories of actions that can follow from this analysis. The analytic categories are as follows.

Tactical threat analysis. Actionable intelligence is essential for preventing acts of terrorism. The timely and thorough analysis and dissemination of information about terrorists and their current and potential activities allow the government to take immediate- and near-term action to disrupt and prevent terrorist acts and to provide useful warning to specific targets, security and public safety professionals, or the general population.

Strategic analysis of the enemy. Our intelligence agencies must have a deep understanding of the organizations that may conduct terrorist attacks against the United States. Knowing the identities, financial and political sources of support, motivation, goals, current and future capabilities, and vulnerabilities of these organizations will assist us in preventing and preempting future attacks, and in taking long-term actions that can weaken support for organizations that seek to damage U.S. interests. Intelligence agencies can support the long-term U.S. strategies to defeat terrorism by understanding the roots of terrorism overseas, and the intentions and capabilities of foreign governments to disrupt terrorist groups in their territories and to assist the United States.

Strategic Analysis of the Enemy Lead: DCI, FBI, DHS

Threat-Vulnerability Integration ("Mapping") Lead: DHS

Vulnerability Assessment Lead: DHS

Tactical Threat Analysis Lead: DCI, FBI, DHS

Warning & Protective Action Lead: DHS

Preventive Action (Tactical) Lead: National JTTF

Strategic Response (Policy)

Long-term Capability Building Lead: OHS

Roles & Responsibilities of Homeland Security Intelligence and Information Analysis *Vulnerability assessments.* Vulnerability assessments must be an integral part of the intelligence cycle for homeland security issues. They allow planners to project the consequences of possible terrorist attacks against specific facilities or different sectors of the economy or government. These projections allow authorities to strengthen defenses against different threats. Such assessments are informed by the use of tools such as computer modeling and analysis.

Threat-Vulnerability integration. Mapping terrorist threats and capabilities—both current and future— against specific facility and sectoral vulnerabilities will allow authorities to determine which organizations pose the greatest threats and which facilities and sectors are most at risk. It will also allow planners to develop thresholds for preemptive or protective action. Figure 1 also depicts three broad categories of action that can result from this analysis.

Tactical preventive action. Analysis can, and must, be turned into action that prevents terrorists from carrying out their plots. The United States has at its disposal numerous tools that allow for the disruption of terrorist acts in the United States and the detention of the terrorists themselves. These tools can be deployed as soon as the analysis uncovers evidence of terrorist planning. This analysis and assessment will help support and enable the actions taken by the U.S. government to prevent terrorism.

Warning and protective action. Inclusive and comprehensive analysis allows the government to take protective action, and to warn appropriate sectors and the public. Defensive action will reduce the potential effectiveness of an attack by prompting relevant sectors to implement security and incident management plans. In addition, defensive action works as a deterrent to terrorists weighing the potential effectiveness of their plans. Warnings allow entities and citizens to take appropriate actions to meet the threat, including upgrading security levels in any affected sectors, activating emergency plans, dispatching state and local law enforcement patrols, and increasing citizen awareness of certain activities.

Strategic response (policy). The enemy of today is far different from those we have faced in the past. The strategies and operating procedures used to fight the traditional strategic threats of the 20th century are of little use in the war on terrorism. We need to develop and create new capabilities specifically designed to defeat the enemy of today and the enemy of the future. This immediate- and long-term strategic capability building will be shaped through budgetary allocations, and will be informed by the careful analysis and assessment of homeland security information. Understanding terrorist organizations will allow policymakers to fashion policies that build international coalitions against terrorism, and eliminate sources of support or sanctuary for terrorists.

Major Initiatives

Enhance the analytic capabilities of the FBI. The Attorney General and the Director of the FBI have established the FBI's top priority as preventing terrorist attacks. They are creating an analytical capability within the FBI that can combine lawfully obtained domestic information with information lawfully derived from investigations, thus facilitating prompt investigation of possible terrorist activity within the United States.

The FBI is instituting several changes as it redefines its mission to focus on preventing terrorist attacks. To

National Vision The collection and analysis of homeland security intelligence and information has become a priority of the highest measure. The intelligence community must enhance its capacity to obtain intelligence relevant to homeland security requirements. The intelligence profession must attract America's brightest and most energetic and allow them to acquire and apply the expertise needed to assure homeland security. In addition, the intelligence community must expand human source intelligence, and develop and utilize technology to enhance analytic, collection, and operational efforts throughout the counterterrorism community.Homeland security intelligence and information must be fed instantaneously into the Nation's domestic anti-terrorism efforts. Those efforts must be structured to provide all pertinent homeland security intelligence and law enforcement information—from all relevant sectors including state and local law enforcement as well as federal agencies—to those able to take preventive or protective action. Under the President's proposal, the new Department will provide real-time actionable information—in the form of protective actions that should be taken in light of terrorist threats, trends, and capabilities, and U.S. vulnerabilities —to policymakers, federal, state, and local law enforcement agencies and the private sector, based on the review and analysis of homeland security information.

To enhance the FBI's analytic capabilities, the Director is seeking to increase the number of staff working to analyze intelligence more than fourfold compared to pre-September 11 figures. The Bureau will hire analysts with specialized expertise, including foreign language capacity, computer skills, and science and engineering backgrounds. The CIA will send approximately 25 of its analysts to the FBI, enhancing not only the FBI's analytical capabilities but also the relationship between these two entities.

Build new capabilities through the Information Analysis and Infrastructure Protection Division of the proposed Department of Homeland Security. The President's proposal to create the Department of Homeland Security would build new and necessary capabilities into the Information Analysis and Infrastructure Protection Division of the Department. Currently, the U.S. government does not perform comprehensive vulnerability assessments of all our Nation's critical infrastructure and key assets. Such vulnerability assessments are important from a planning perspective in that they enable authorities to evaluate the potential effects of an attack on a given facility or sector, and then to invest accordingly in protecting such facilities and sectors. The Department of Homeland Security would have the responsibility and capability of performing these comprehensive vulnerability assessments. (See *Protecting Critical Infrastructure and Key Assets* chapter for additional discussion.)

The vulnerability assessments, important in their own right, are also building blocks for a key homeland security function that currently is not being performed: threat-vulnerability integration. Today, no government entity is responsible for analyzing terrorist threats to the homeland, mapping those threats against our vulnerabilities, and taking protective action. Our intelligence and federal law enforcement agencies focus on the detection and disruption of each individual threat. The Department of Homeland Security, informed by intelligence and information analysis and vulnerability assessments, would focus on longer-term protective measures, such as the setting of priorities for critical infrastructure protection and "targethardening." (See *Protecting Critical Infrastructure and Key Assets* chapter for additional discussion.)

To perform this function, the Secretary of the new Department of Homeland Security would have broad statutory authority to access intelligence information, as well as other types of information, relevant to the terrorist threat to our Nation. Indeed, the President's proposal not only permits, but requires, each executive agency to promptly provide the Secretary all reports, assessments, and analytical information relating to the missions of the new Department. The Department would also work with state and local law enforcement and the private sector to leverage the critical homeland security information in the possession of these entities. In addition to transforming homeland security information into long-term protective action, the Department of Homeland Security would also turn the information into useful warnings. The Department would serve as the primary provider of threat information to state and local public safety agencies and to private sector owners of key targets, thereby minimizing confusion, gaps and duplication. The combination of these new capabilities within the Department of Homeland Security and the existing and enhanced capabilities of our Nation's intelligence and law enforcement communities would enable the federal government to combat terrorism with maximum effect.

Implement the Homeland Security Advisory System. The Homeland Security Advisory System disseminates information regarding the risk of terrorist acts to federal, state, and local authorities, the private sector and the American people. The Advisory System creates a common vocabulary, context, and structure for the ongoing national discussion about the nature of the threats that confront the homeland and the appropriate measures that should be taken in response. It seeks to inform and facilitate decisions appropriate to different levels of government and to private citizens at home and at work. The Department of Homeland Security would be responsible for managing the Advisory System.

The Advisory System provides a national framework for public announcements of threat advisories and alerts to notify law enforcement and state and local government officials of threats. They serve to inform the public about government preparations, and to provide the public with the information necessary to respond to the threat. The Advisory System characterizes appropriate levels of vigilance, preparedness, and readiness in a series of graduated threat conditions. Each threat condition has corresponding suggested measures to be taken in response. Such responses include increasing surveillance of critical locations, preparing to execute contingency procedures, and closing public and government facilities.

Utilize dual-use analysis to prevent attacks. Terrorists use equipment and materials to carry out their criminal acts. Such equipment and material can include items such as fermenters, aerosol generators, protective gear, antibiotics, and disease-causing agents. Many of these items are "dual-use" items—they have not just terrorist applications, but also legitimate commercial applications, and can often be bought on the open market. If suspect dual-use acquisitions are identified, crossreferenced with intelligence and law enforcement databases, and mapped against threat analyses, the U.S. government's ability to detect terrorist activities at the preparation stage will be enhanced. Therefore, the federal government, led by the Department of Homeland Security, will evaluate and study mechanisms through which suspect purchases of dual-use equipment and materials can be reported and analyzed. (See *Defending against Catastrophic Threats* chapter for a discussion of the Select Agent Program.)

Employ "red team" techniques. The Department of Homeland Security, working with the intelligence community, would utilize "red team" techniques to improve and focus of the Nation's defenses against terrorism. Applying homeland security intelligence and information, the new Department would have certain employees responsible for viewing the United States from the perspective of the terrorists, seeking to discern and predict the methods, means and targets of the terrorists. Today's enemies do not think and act in the same manner as yesterday's. The new Department would use its capabilities and analysis to learn how they think in order to set priorities for long-term protective action and "target hardening." Employing "red team" tactics, the new Department would seek to uncover weaknesses in the security measures at our Nation's critical infrastructure sectors during government-sponsored exercises. (See *Protecting Critical Infrastructure and Key Assets* chapter for additional discussion.)

CHAPTER 6
Border and Transportation Security

The United States shares a 5,525 mile border with Canada and a 1,989 mile border with Mexico. Our maritime border includes 95,000 miles of shoreline and navigable waterways as well as a 3.4 million square mile exclusive economic zone. All people and goods legally entering into the United States must be processed through an air, land, or sea port of entry. Many international airports are dispersed throughout the United States. Each year, more than 500 million people legally enter our country. Some 330 million are non-citizens; more than 85 percent enter via land borders, often as daily commuters. An enormous volume of trade also crosses our borders every day— some $1.35 trillion in imports and $1 trillion in exports were processed in 2001.

America historically has relied heavily on two vast oceans and two friendly neighbors for border security, and on the private sector for most forms of domestic transportation security. The increasing mobility and destructive potential of modern terrorism has required the United States to rethink and rearrange fundamentally its systems for border and transportation security. Indeed, we must now begin to conceive of border security and transportation security as fully integrated requirements because our domestic transportation systems are intertwined inextricably with the global transport infrastructure. Virtually every community in America is connected to the global transportation network by the seaports, airports, highways, pipelines, railroads, and waterways that move people and goods into, within, and out of the Nation. We therefore must promote the efficient and reliable flow of people, goods, and services across borders, while preventing terrorists from using transportation conveyances or systems to deliver implements of destruction.

Major Initiatives

Ensure accountability in border and transportation security. The

President has proposed to Congress that the principal border and transportation security agencies—the Immigration and Naturalization Service, U.S. Customs Service, U.S. Coast Guard, Animal and Plant Health Inspection Service, and Transportation Security Agency—be transferred to the new Department of Homeland Security. The new Department also would control the issuance of visas to foreigners through the Department of State and would coordinate the border-control activities of all federal agencies that are not incorporated within the new Department.

Create "smart borders." Our future border management system will be radically different from today's which focuses on linear borders. It will create a "border of the future" that will be a continuum framed by land, sea, and air dimensions, where a layered management system enables greater visibility of vehicles, people, and goods coming to and departing from our country. This border of the future will provide greater security through better intelligence, coordinated national efforts, and unprecedented international cooperation against the threats posed by terrorists, the implements of terrorism, international organized crime, illegal drugs, illegal migrants, cyber crime, and the destruction or theft of natural resources. At the same time, the border of the future will be increasingly transparent to the efficient flow of people, goods, and conveyances engaged in legitimate economic and social activities. The federal government will allocate resources in a balanced way to manage risk in our border and transportation security systems while ensuring the expedient flow of goods, services, and people. Internationally, the United States will seek to screen and verify the security of goods and identities of people before they can harm to the international transportation system and well before they reach our shores or land borders.

The Department of Homeland Security would improve information provided to consular officers so that individual applicants can be checked in comprehensive databases and would require visa-issuance procedures to reflect threat assessments. The United States will require visitors to present travel documentation that includes biometric identifiers. The United States will also work with international organizations and the private sector to improve the security of people, goods, conveyances traveling internationally, and the ports that they use. The United States will work with other countries and international organizations to improve the quality of travel documents and their issuance to minimize their misuse by smugglers and terrorist organizations.We will also assist other countries, as appropriate, to improve their border controls and their coordination with us. Finally, we will work closely with Canada and Mexico to increase the security of our shared borders while facilitating commerce within the North American Free Trade Agreement (NAFTA) area.

At our borders, the Department of Homeland Security would verify and process the entry of people in order to prevent the entrance of contraband, unauthorized aliens, and potential terrorists. The Department would increase the information available on inbound goods and passengers so that border management agencies can apply risk-based management tools. The Department would develop and deploy the statutorily required entry-exit system to record the arrival and departure of foreign visitors and guests. It would develop and deploy non-intrusive inspection technologies to ensure rapid and more thorough screening of goods and conveyances. And it would monitor all our borders in order to detect illegal intrusions and intercept and apprehend smuggled goods and people attempting to enter illegally.

National Vision

A single entity in the Department of Homeland Security will manage who and what enters our homeland in order to prevent the entry of terrorists and the instruments of terror while facilitating the legal flow of people, goods, and services on which our economy depends. The Department and its partners will conduct bordersecurity functions abroad to the extent allowed by technology and international agreements. Federal law enforcement agencies will take swift action against those who introduce contraband or violate terms of entry and pose threats to the American people. The U.S. government will work with the international community and the private sector to secure the transportation systems which link American communities to the world, moving people and goods across our borders and throughout the country within hours.

The Department of Homeland Security proposed by the President will also build an immigration services.organization that administers immigration laws in an efficient, expeditious, fair, and humane manner. The Department would ensure that foreign visitors comply with entry conditions. The Department, in cooperation with colleges and universities, would track and monitor international students and exchange visitors. The Department would enter into national law enforcement databases the names of high-risk aliens who remain in the United States longer than authorized and, when warranted, deport illegal aliens.

Increase the security of international shipping containers. Containers are an indispensable but vulnerable link in the chain of global trade; approximately 90 percent of the world's cargo moves by container. Each year, nearly 50 percent of the value of all U.S. imports arrives via 16 million containers. The core elements of this initiative are to establish security criteria to identify high-risk containers; pre-screen containers before they arrive at U.S. ports; use technology to inspect high-risk containers; and develop and use smart and secure containers. The United States will place inspectors at foreign seaports to screen U.S.-bound sea containers before they are shipped to America, initially focusing on the top 20 "mega" ports (including Rotterdam, Antwerp, and Le Havre), because roughly 68 percent of the 5.7 million sea containers entering the United States annually arrive from these seaports.

Implement the Aviation and Transportation Security Act of 2001. On November 19, 2001, the President signed into law the Aviation and Transportation Security Act of 2001. The act established a series of challenging but important milestones toward achieving a secure air travel system. More broadly, however, the act fundamentally changed the way transportation security will be performed and managed in the United States. The continued growth of the world economy—and, in particular, commercial transportation and tourism— depends upon effective transportation security measures being efficiently applied. The act recognized the importance of security for all forms of transportation and related infrastructure elements. This cannot be accomplished by the federal government in isolation and requires strengthened partnerships among federal, state, and local government officials and the private sector to reduce vulnerabilities and adopt the best practices available today. Protection of critical transportation assets such as ports, pipelines, rail, and highway bridges, and more than 10,000 FAA facilities is another key requirement established by the act. Additionally, the Transportation Security Administration will coordinate federal efforts to secure the national airspace—an essential medium for travel, commerce, and recreation.

The federal government will work with the private sector to upgrade security in all modes of transportation.

Areas of emphasis will include: commercial aviation and other mass transportation systems; intermodal transportation; hazardous and explosive materials; national airspace; shipping container security; traffic-management systems; critical infrastructure; surety of transportation operators and workers; linkages with international transportation systems; and information sharing. We will utilize existing modal relationships and systems to implement unified, national standards for transportation security.

Recapitalize the U.S. Coast Guard. The Budget for Fiscal Year 2003 requested the largest increase in the history of the U.S. Coast Guard. The Budget for Fiscal Year 2004 will continue to support the recapitalization of the U.S. Coast Guard's aging fleet, as well as targeted improvements in the areas of maritime domain awareness, command and control systems, and shore-side facilities. The United States asks much of its U.S. Coast Guard and we will ensure the service has the resources needed to accomplish its multiple missions. We saw the dedication and the versatility of the U.S. Coast Guard in the aftermath of September 11, a performance that vividly demonstrated the U.S. Coast Guard's vital contribution to homeland security. Nevertheless, the U.S. Coast Guard is also responsible for national defense, maritime safety, maritime mobility, and protection of natural resources, and would continue to fulfill these functions in the Department of Homeland Security.

Reform immigration services. The Administration will complete reform of the Immigration and Naturalization Service (INS), separating the agency's enforcement and service functions within, as the President has proposed, the new Department of Homeland Security. This reform aims to ensure full enforcement of the laws that regulate the admission of aliens to the United States and to improve greatly the administration of immigration benefits to more than 7 million annual applicants. Americans have long cherished our identity as a nation of immigrants. This reform will ensure that every applicant's case is reviewed in a timely and courteous way. Finally, the Department of Homeland Security would implement the Enhanced Border Security and Visa Entry Reform Act, including the requirement that foreign visitors possess travel documents with biometric information.

The attacks of September 11 and the catastrophic loss of life and property that resulted have redefined the mission of federal, state, and local law enforcement authorities. While law enforcement agencies will continue to investigate and prosecute criminal activity, they should now assign priority to preventing and interdicting terrorist activity within the United States. Effectively reorienting law enforcement organizations to focus on counterterrorism objectives requires decisive action in a number of areas. Many of the necessary steps have already been taken, although additional work remains to be done before law enforcement agencies collectively can pursue the counterterrorism mission with maximum effect. The federal government has already instituted initiatives that have increased information sharing and the coordination of operations throughout the law enforcement community. Not only are the federal law enforcement and U.S. intelligence agencies communicating better with each other, the entire law enforcement community—international, federal, state, and local—is now sharing more information. In addition, law enforcement agencies at all levels of government have worked to enhance coordination of their counterterrorism operational activities so that our collective efforts complement each other.

CHAPTER 7
Domestic Counterterrorism

While the intelligence and law enforcement communities have made progress in the areas of information sharing and coordination, major shortcomings continue to exist in other important areas. Our government's ability to identify key sources of funding for terrorist activity and the methods used to finance terrorist operations remains inadequate. The U.S. government has not yet developed a satisfactory system to analyze information in order to predict and assess the threat of a terrorist attack within the United States. The federal government needs to do a better job of utilizing the distinct capabilities of state and local law enforcement to prevent terrorism by giving them access, where appropriate, to the information in our federal databases, and by utilizing state and local information at the federal level. The FBI-led Joint Terrorism Task Forces, by including participants from state and local law enforcement as well as federal agencies, draw on state and local capabilities, and enhance intergovernmental coordination.

Major Initiatives

Several chapters, such as *Intelligence and Warning, Border and Transportation Security*, and *Protecting Critical Infrastructure and Key Assets*, are closely interrelated with *Domestic Counterterrorism*. (See, for example, "Tactical Preventive Action" in the *Intelligence and Warning* chapter.) This chapter only discusses counterterrorism initiatives and actions that do not fall under other critical mission areas.

Improve intergovernmental law enforcement coordination. An effective domestic counterterrorism effort requires the participation of law enforcement personnel at all levels of government, as well as the coordination of all relevant agencies and officials. Toward this end, the FBI is expanding the Joint Terrorism Task Forces (JTTFs), now operating in 47 field offices, to all 56 FBI field offices by August 2002. The Task Forces have primary operational responsibility for terrorism investigations that are not related to ongoing prosecutions. The JTTFs, whose participants represent numerous federal agencies and state and local law enforcement, combine the national and international investigative capacity of the federal government with the state and local "on-the-beat" knowledge and capabilities.

Facilitate apprehension of potential terrorists. In order to apprehend suspected terrorists before they have the opportunity to execute their plans, we must ensure that law enforcement officers are able to access information on suspected terrorists. Several initiatives are underway to create fully accessible sources of information relating to suspected terrorists. First, the Department of Justice has expanded and will continue to expand the data included in the FBI's National Crime Information Center (NCIC) database, which is accessible to approximately 650,000 state and local law enforcement officers. The names and identifying information of subjects of domestic and foreign terrorism investigations have already been entered into the database. The Department of Justice is adding to the NCIC database the names of over 300,000 fugitive aliens in violation of final orders of deportation. In addition, the Attorney General has directed the FBI to establish procedures with the Department of State to enable inclusion of data from the TIPOFF System—which provides information on known or suspected terrorists to immigration and consular officers—into the NCIC database. The ultimate objective of this effort is to ensure that the "cop on the beat" has access to pertinent information regarding potential terrorists.

The FBI is also establishing a consolidated terrorism watch list that will serve as a central access point for information about individuals of investigative interest. The watch list will be fully accessible to the law enforcement and intelligence communities, and will include information derived from FBI and Joint Terrorism Task Force investigations, the intelligence community, the Department of Defense, and foreign governments.

The Attorney General has directed the FBI, through its Legal Attaches, to establish procedures to obtain fingerprints, other identifying information, and available biographical data of all known or suspected terrorists who have been identified and processed by foreign law enforcement agencies, and to enter such data into the FBI's Integrated Automated Fingerprint Identification System and other appropriate databases. The Attorney General has also modified certain guidelines to give the FBI greater latitude to conduct

National Vision

We will redefine our law enforcement mission to focus on the prevention of all terrorist acts within the United States, whether international or domestic in origin. We will use all legal means— both traditional and non-traditional—to identify, halt, and, where appropriate, prosecute terrorists in the United States. We will prosecute or bring immigration or other civil charges against such individuals where appropriate and will utilize the full range of our legal authorities. We will pursue not only the individuals directly engaged in terrorist activity, but also their sources of support: the people and organizations that knowingly fund the terrorists and those that provide them with logistical assistance. To achieve these aims, we will strengthen our federal law enforcement community. In addition, we will augment the scope and quality of information available to all law enforcement. In that regard, we will build and continually update a fully integrated, fully accessible terrorist watch list. When we have identified any suspected terrorist activities, we will then use all the tools in our Nation's legal arsenal, including investigative, criminal, civil, immigration, and regulatory powers to stop those who wish to do us harm.

We must continue to do essential counterterrorism investigative activities in the United States, and to utilize commercially available computer databases in support of counterterrorism investigations, consistent with Constitutional standards. Such databases serve a key function in the effort to apprehend suspected terrorists before they carry out any terrorist act as the data contained therein can reveal patterns of criminal behavior. The Department of Justice currently is engaged in "datamining" projects that utilize computer technology to analyze information to reveal patterns of behavior consistent with terrorist activities. For example, utilizing law enforcement and intelligence information as well as public source data, the Foreign Terrorist Tracking Task Force employs risk modeling algorithms, link analysis, historic review of past patterns of behavior, and other factors to distinguish persons who may pose a risk of terrorism from those who do not.

Continue ongoing investigations and prosecutions. The Nation's law enforcement community currently is investigating both confirmed and suspected terrorist activity. The largest and most extensive investigation is "Penttbom"—the FBI's inquiry into the attacks of September 11. "Penttbom" is the largest criminal investigation in history, currently involving the cooperation of numerous federal agencies, state and local law enforcement, and the intelligence and law enforcement agencies of foreign countries. Several prosecutions are now underway as a result of the "Penttbom" investigation, including the prosecution of Zacarias Moussaoui on charges of conspiring with Osama bin Laden and others to carry out the attacks of September 11.

Our counterterrorism efforts also include the investigation and prosecution of foreign and domestic terrorists unrelated to the September 11 attacks, as well as the pursuit of individuals who provide logistical support to terrorists. In addition, law enforcement agencies are pursuing a more aggressive preventive strategy by investigating and dismantling criminal rings throughout the country that sell false driver's licenses, certifications for the transportation of hazardous materials, passports, and visas. As the chief federal law enforcement officer, the Attorney General—relying heavily on the FBI—will lead federal law enforcement efforts in investigations and prosecutions, while coordinating with the Department of Homeland Security and other federal law enforcement agencies, as well as state and local authorities. State and local law enforcement personnel, operating within each community, are indispensable to our domestic counterterrorism efforts, playing several critical roles, including uncovering and reporting unusual behavior and security anomalies.

Complete FBI restructuring to emphasize prevention of terrorist attacks. Our Nation's highest law enforcement objective must be the prevention of terrorist acts—a significant shift from pre-September 11 objectives. In order to focus the mission of the federal law enforcement community on prevention, the federal government, working with Congress, needs to restructure the FBI and other federal law enforcement agencies, reallocating certain resources and energies to the new prevention efforts.

The FBI already has made several structural changes to reflect the primacy of the counterterrorism mission. For example, in the fall of 2001, the Director of the FBI established new positions responsible for strengthening information sharing and coordination with state and local law enforcement agencies. The FBI Director recently announced the second phase of the reorganization, under which significant resources will be committed to preventing terrorist attacks, pending congressional approval. The plan increases the FBI's counterterrorism investigative capabilities and flexibility by shifting hundreds of field agents from criminal investigations to counterterrorism investigations and activities. At the same time, this shift allows each field office to meet national programmatic objectives for the FBI's highest priority— preventing terrorist attacks within the United States.

The plan also seeks to build within the FBI a concentrated, national, centralized, and deployable expertise on terrorism issues. This requires both ensuring that information and knowledge in the field offices gets relayed to headquarters and creating expertise that can be easily accessed by and deployed to field offices. In order to respond to the need for a more flexible and mobile deployment of highly knowledgeable counterterrorism agents, the FBI plans to devote a portion of the increased personnel to "Flying Squads." These squads, consisting of agents with specific counterterrorism expertise, will travel to field offices when their expertise is needed, and will bring valuable information back to FBI headquarters for analysis. Reflecting the global nature of the terrorist reality, the "Flying Squads" will also be deployed overseas when necessary. In addition, the FBI will augment its overseas presence and partnerships by increasing the number of Legal Attaches around the world, who will fall under the authority of our Ambassadors.

The plan also includes the establishment of a new, expansive multi-agency National Joint Terrorism Task Force at FBI Headquarters that will complement the Joint Terrorism Task Forces established in local FBI field offices and improve collaboration and information sharing with other agencies. (See *Intelligence and Warning* chapter for additional discussion on FBI restructuring.)

Target and attack terrorist financing. A cornerstone of our counterterrorism effort is a concerted interagency effort to target and interdict financing of terrorist operations. The FBI's Financial Review Group and Operation Green Quest at the U.S. Customs Service, proposed to be a component of the Department of Homeland Security, have spearheaded the enforcement component of the terrorist finance interdiction effort. The Review Group is a multi-agency effort led by the FBI to investigate suspicious financial transactions in order to uncover and prosecute terrorist financing and develop predictive models to help identify future illegal financing. Operation Green Quest, launched by the Department of Treasury at the Customs Service, works to freeze the accounts of, and seize the assets of, individuals and organizations that finance terrorist groups. Going forward, the FBI should lead the federal government law enforcement campaign against terrorist financing, with support from the Department of Homeland Security.

Track foreign terrorists and bring them to justice. The federal government has two key missions in regard to tracking foreign terrorists: barring terrorists or terrorist-supporting aliens from the United States and tracking down and deporting any who have illegally entered our country. The Foreign Terrorist Tracking Task Force at the Department of Justice currently performs this function. The Task Force is also charged with facilitating coordination and communication among the agencies with immigration and enforcement responsibilities.

Terrorists are opportunistic. They exploit vulnerabilities we leave exposed, choosing the time, place, and method of attack according to the weaknesses they observe or perceive. Increasing the security of a particular type of target, such as aircraft or buildings, makes it more likely that terrorists will seek a different target. Increasing the counter-measures to a particular terrorist tactic, such as hijacking, makes it more likely that terrorists will favor a different tactic. Protecting America's critical infrastructure and key assets is thus a formidable challenge. Our open and technologically complex society presents an almost infinite array of potential targets, and our critical infrastructure changes as rapidly as the marketplace. It is impossible to protect completely all targets, all the time. On the other hand, we can help deter or deflect attacks, or mitigate their effects, by making strategic improvements in protection and security. Thus, while we cannot assume we will prevent all terrorist attacks, we can substantially reduce America's vulnerability, particularly to the most damaging attacks.

CHAPTER 8
Protecting Critical Infrastructures and Key Assets

All elements of our society have a crucial stake in reducing our vulnerability to terrorism; and all have highly valuable roles to play. Protecting America's critical infrastructure and key assets requires an unprecedented level of cooperation throughout all levels of government-with private industry and institutions, and with the American people. The federal government has the crucial task of fostering a collaborative environment, and enabling all of these entities to work together to provide America the security it requires.

What must we protect? The USA PATRIOT Act defines critical infrastructure as those "systems and assets, whether physical or virtual, so vital to the United States that the incapacity or destruction of such systems and assets would have a debilitating impact on security, national economic security, national public health or safety, or any combination of those matters." Our critical infrastructures are particularly important because of the functions or services they provide to our country. Our critical infrastructures are also particularly important because they are complex systems: the effects of a terrorist attack can spread far beyond the direct target, and reverberate long after the immediate damage.

America's critical infrastructure encompasses a large number of sectors. Our agriculture, food, and water sectors, along with the public health and emergency services sectors, provide the essential goods and services Americans need to survive. Our institutions of government guarantee our national security and freedom, and administer key public functions. Our defense industrial base provides essential capabilities to help safeguard our population from external threats. Our information and telecommunications sector enables economic productivity and growth, and is particularly important because it connects and helps control many other infrastructure sectors. Our energy, transportation, banking and finance, chemical industry, and postal and shipping sectors help sustain our economy and touch the lives of Americans everyday.

The assests, functions, and systems within each critical infrastructure sector are not equally important. The transportation sector is vital, but not every bridge is critical to the Nation as a whole. Accordingly, the federal government will apply a consistent methodology to focus its effort on the highest priorities, and the federal budget will differentiate resources required for critical infrastructure protection from resources required for other important protection activities. The federal government will work closely with state and local governments to develop and apply compatible approaches to ensure protection for critical assests, systems, and functions at all levels of society. For example, local schools, courthouses, and bridges are critical to the communities they serve.

Protecting America's critical infrastructure and key assests requires more than just resources. The federal government can use a broad range of measures to help enable state, local, and private sector entities to better protect the assests and infrastructures they control. For example, the government can create venues to share information on infrastructure vulnerabilities and bestpractice solutions, or create a more effective means of providing specific and useful threat information to non-federal entities in a timely fashion. In addition to our critical infrastructure, our country must also protect a number of key assets—individual targets whose destruction would not endanger vital systems, but could create local disaster or profoundly damage our Nation's morale or confidence. Key assets include symbols or historical attractions, such as prominent national, state, or local monuments and icons. In some cases, these include quasi-public symbol that are identified strongly with the United States as a Nation, and fall completely under the jurisdiction of state and local officials or even private foundations. Key assets also include individual or localized facilities that deserve special protection because of their destructive potential or their value to the local community.

Finally, certain high-profile events are strongly coupled to our national symbols or national morale and deserve special protective efforts by the federal government.

Critical Infrastructure Sectors

Agriculture

Food

Water

Public Health

Emergency Services

Government

Defense Industrial Base

Information and Telecommunications

Energy

Transportation

Banking and Finance

Chemical Industry

Postal and Shipping

Major Initiatives

Unify America's infrastructure protection effort in the Department of Homeland Security. Our country requires a single accountable official to ensure we address vulnerabilities that involve more than one infrastructure sector or require action by more than one agency. Our country also requires a single accountable official to assess threats and vulnerabilities comprehensively across all infrastructure sectors to ensure we reduce the overall risk to our country, instead of inadvertently shifting risk from one potential set of targets to another. Under the President's proposal, the Department of Homeland Security will assume responsibility for integrating and coordinating federal infrastructure protection responsibilities.

The Department of Homeland Security would consolidate and focus the activities performed by the Critical Infrastructure Assurance Office (currently part of the Department of Commerce) and the National Infrastructure Protection Center (FBI), less those portions that investigate computer crime. The Department would augment those capabilities with the Federal Computer Incident Response Center (General Services Administration), the Computer Security Division of the National Institute of Standards and Technology (Commerce), and the National Communications System (Defense).

The Department of Homeland Security would also unify the responsibility for coordinating cyber and physical infrastructure protection efforts. Currently, the federal government divides responsibility for cyber and physical infrastructure, and key cyber security activities are scattered in multiple departments.While securing cyberspace poses unique challenges and issues, requiring unique tools and solutions, our physical and cyber infrastructures are interconnected. The devices that control our physical systems, including our electrical distribution system, transportation systems, dams, and other important infrastructure, are increasingly connected to the Internet. Thus, the consequences of an attack on our cyber infrastructure can cascade across many sectors. Moreover, the number, virulence, and maliciousness of cyber attacks have increased dramatically in recent years. Accordingly, under the President's proposal, the Department of Homeland Security will place an especially high priority on protecting our cyber infrastructure. Reducing America's vulnerability to terrorism must also harness the coordinated effort of many federal departments and agencies that have highly specialized expertise and long-standing relationships with industry.

For example, the Treasury Department chairs the Financial and Banking Information Infrastructure Committee, which brings together several federal agencies and the private sector to focus on issues related to the financial services industry. Each of the critical infrastructure sectors has unique characteristics, hence posing unique security challenges. The Department of Homeland Security would coordinate the activities of the federal departments and agencies to address the unique security challenges of each infrastructure sector. The following chart depicts the federal government's organization for protecting America's infrastructure and key assests, and indicates the departments and agencies that have primary responsibility for interacting with particular critical infrastructure sectors.

National Vision

The United States will forge an unprecedented level of cooperation throughout all levels of government, with private industry and institutions, and with the American people to protect our critical infrastructure and key assets from terrorist attack. Our country will continue to take immediate and decisive action to protect assets and systems that could be attacked with catastrophic consequences. We will establish a single office within the Department of Homeland Security to work with the federal departments and agencies, state and local governments, and the private sector to implement a comprehensive national plan to protect critical infrastructure and key assets. The national infrastructure protection plan will organize the complementary efforts of government and private institutions to raise security over the long term to levels appropriate to each target's vulnerability and criticality. The federal government will work to create an environment in which state, local, and private entities can best protect the infrastructure they control. The Department of Homeland Security will develop the best modeling and simulation tools to understand how our increasingly complex and connected infrastructures behave, and to shape effective protection and response options. The Department of Homeland Security will develop and coordinate implementation of tiered protective measures that can be tailored to the target and rapidly adjusted to the threat. The Department of Homeland Security, working through the Department of State, will foster international cooperation to protect shared and interconnected infrastructure.

Federal Government Organizations will Protect Critical Infrastructure and Key Assets, lead by the President and the Secretary of Homeland Security

They will take care of federal, state, local, and private sector coordination and integration and comprehensive national infrastructure protection plan plus mapping threats to vulnerabilities and issuing warnings

Agriculture: Department of Agriculture

Food: *Meat and poultry* Department of Agriculture

All other food products Department of Health & Human Services

Water: Environmental Protection Agency

Public Health: Department of Health & Human Services

Emergency Services: Department of Homeland Security

Government:

Continuity of government Department of Homeland Security

Continuity of operations All departments and agencies

Defense Industrial Base: Department of Defense

Information and Telecommunications: Department of Homeland Security

Energy:

 Department of Energy Transportation

Department of Homeland Security*

Banking and Finance: Department of the Treasury

Chemical Industry and Hazardous Materials: Environmental Protection Agency

Postal and Shipping :Department of Homeland Security

National Monuments and Icons: Department of the Interior

* Under the President's proposal, the Transportation Security Administration, responsible for securing our Nation's transportation systems, will become part of the Department of Homeland Security. The new Department will coordinate closely with the Department of Transportation, which will remain responsible for transportation safety.

Build and maintain a complete and accurate assessment of America's critical infrastructure and key assets. The Department of Homeland Security must be able to translate threat information into appropriate action in the shortest possible time, a critical factor in preventing or mitigating attacks, particularly those involving weapons of mass destruction. Accordingly, the Department would build and maintain a complete, current, and accurate assessment of vulnerabilities and preparedness of critical targets across critical infrastructure sectors. The Department would thus have a crucial capability that does not exist in our government today: the ability to continuously evaluate threat information against our current vulnerabilities, inform the President, issue warnings, and effect action accordingly. As noted in the *Intelligence and Warning* chapter, the Department would augment this unique capability with "red team" techniques to view our vulnerabilities from the perspective of terrorists, and to provide objective data on which to base infrastructure protection standards and performance measures.

A complete and thorough assessment of America's vulnerabilities will not only enable decisive near-term action, but guide the rational long-term investment of effort and resources. For example, a comprehensive assessment of vulnerabilities and threats can help determine whether to invest in permanent, physical "hardening" of a target, or in maintaining a reserve of personnel and equipment that can meet a temporary "surge" requirement for increased security.

Enable effective partnership with state and local governments and the private sector. Government at the federal, state, and local level must actively collaborate and partner with the private sector, which controls 85 percent of America's infrastructure. Private firms bear primary and substantial responsibility for addressing the public safety risks posed by their industriesprotecting a firm's assets and systems is a matter of sound corporate governance. In many cases private firms, not the government, possess the technical expertise and means to protect the infrastructure they control. Government at all levels must enable, not inhibit, the private sector's ability to carry out its protection responsibilities. The Nation's infrastructure protection effort must harness the capabilities of the private sector to achieve a prudent level of security without hindering productivity, trade, or economic growth.

The Department of Homeland Security would give state and local agencies and the private sector one primary contact instead of many for coordinating protection activities with the federal government, including vulnerability assessments, strategic planning efforts, and exercises. The Department would include an office which reports directly to the Secretary dedicated to this function, and would build on current outreach efforts of existing federal agencies with infrastructure protection responsibilities.

When the Department of Homeland Security learns of a potential threat to our critical infrastructure, it must not only disseminate warnings quickly, but must rapidly map those threats against an accurate assessment of our country's vulnerabilities and effect appropriate action. To ensure this, the government must facilitate and encourage private firms to share important information about the infrastructure they control. Private firms should have reasonable assurance that good faith disclosures about vulnerabilities and preparedness do not expose the firm to liability, drops in share value, loss of competitive advantage, or antitrust action. As discussed in the *Law* chapter, the Attorney General will convene a panel to propose any legal changes necessary to enable sharing of essential homeland security related information between the government and the private sector.

Develop a national infrastructure protection plan. The Department of Homeland Security would develop and coordinate implementation of a comprehensive national plan to protect America's infrastructure from terrorist attack. The plan will build on the baseline physical and cyber infrastructure protection plans which the Office of Homeland Security and the President's Critical Infrastructure Protection Board will release by the end of Fiscal Year 2002. The national plan will provide a methodology for identifying and prioritizing critical assets, systems, and functions, and for sharing protection responsibility with state and local government and the private sector. The plan will establish standards and benchmarks for infrastructure protection, and provide a means to measure performance. The plan will inform the Department of Homeland Security's annual process for planning, programming, and budgeting of critical infrastructure protection activities, including research and development. As discussed in the *Costs of Homeland Security* chapter, the national infrastructure protection plan will also provide an approach for rationally balancing the costs and benefits of increased security according to the threat—to help answer, in effect, "how much protection is enough?" The plan will describe how to use all available policy instruments to raise the security of America's critical infrastructure and key assets to a prudent level, relying to the maximum possible extent on the market to provide appropriate levels of security. The Department would manage federal grant programs for homeland security, which may be used to assist state and local infrastructure protection efforts. In some cases, the Department may seek legislation to create incentives for the private sector to adopt security measures or invest in improved safety technologies. In other cases, the federal government will need to rely on regulation—for example, to require commercial airlines to electronically transmit passenger manifests on international flights, or to require permits for intrastate purchase of explosives.

Securing cyberspace. The cost to our economy from attacks on our information systems has grown by 400 percent in four years according to one estimate, but is still limited. In one day, however, that could change. Every day somewhere in America an individual company or a home computer user suffers what for them are significantly damaging or catastrophic losses from cyber attacks. The ingredients are present for that kind of damage to occur on a national level, to our national networks and the systems they run upon, on which the nation depends. Our potential enemies have the intent; the tools of destruction are broadly available; the vulnerabilities of our systems are myriad and well-known. In cyberspace, a single act can inflict damage in multiple locations simultaneously without the attacker ever having physically entered the United States.

Accordingly, the President acted quickly following the terrorist attacks in September to secure our information and telecommunications infrastructure. The President created the Critical Infrastructure Protection Board and launched a public-private partnership to create a *National Strategy to Secure Cyberspace.* The *National Strategy to Secure Cyberspace* will provide a roadmap to empower all Americans to secure the part of cyberspace they control, including a variety of new proposals aimed at five levels: the home user and small business; large enterprises; sectors of the economy; national issues; and global issues.

Thousands of citizens all across the country have contributed to the effort by contributing their views in Town Hall meetings, on interactive web sites, or by participating in one of the dozens of participating groups and associations. State and local governments and state and local law enforcement have also united to prepare their own cyber security strategies.

Harness the best analytic and modeling tools to develop effective protective solutions. As discussed in the *Intelligence and Warning* chapter, responding to threat information requires life-or-death decisions that must often be made in conditions of great uncertainty. Highend modeling and simulation tools can greatly enhance our ability to quickly make those decisions based on the best possible understanding of their consequences. State-of-the-art modeling and simulation provides another important tool for determining what assets, systems, and functions are "critical," a process that involves many factors that interact with one another in complex ways. For example, an attack on a key Internet node might cause few casualties directly, but could trigger cascading effects across many infrastructure sectors, causing widespread disruption to the economy and imperiling public safety. An attack on a major port could inflict damage that affects transportation, energy, and economic infrastructure nationwide. A chemical attack would have little effect on an empty stadium; a catastrophic effect on a stadium filled with tens of thousands of spectators. Protecting America's critical infrastructure thus requires that we determine the highest risks based on the best possible understanding of these factors, and prioritize our effort accordingly.

The Department of Homeland Security would develop and harness the best modeling, simulation, and analytic tools to evaluate the full range of relevant factors and the complex manner in which they interact. The Department would take as its foundation the National Infrastructure Simulation and Analysis Center (currently part of the Department of Energy).

Guard America's critical infrastructure and key assets against "inside" threats. The "insider threat" and personnel reliability are increasingly serious concerns for protecting critical infrastructure. In the food processing and distribution industry, disgruntled or former employees have caused nearly all previous incidents of food tampering, providing a glimpse of what terrorists with insider access might accomplish. Personnel with privileged access to critical infrastructure, particularly control systems, may serve as terrorist surrogates by providing information on vulnerabilities, operating characteristics, and protective measures. These "insiders" can also provide access to sensitive areas, such as loading docks, control centers, and airport tarmacs. The U.S. government, working through the Department of Homeland Security will undertake a comprehensive review of critical infrastructure personnel surety programs and propose national standards for screening and background checks. To this end, the Secretary of Homeland Security and the Attorney General will convene a panel with appropriate representatives from federal, state, and local government, in consultation with the private sector, to examine whether employer liability statutes and privacy concerns hinder necessary background checks of personnel with access to critical infrastructure facilities or systems. The Department of Homeland Security would also undertake a comprehensive review of other protection measures necessary to deny terrorist access to critical infrastructure—for example, establishing "security zones" and controlling access around vulnerable port facilities much as we control access at airports.

Partner with the international community to protect our transnational infrastructure. We share much of our critical infrastructure with our neighbors in Canada and Mexico, and increasingly with countries around the world. Our electricity transmission, natural gas and petroleum pipelines are part of a vast, interconnected system that serves not only the United States, but Canada and Mexico as well. America's seaports often contain dense concentrations of population and critical infrastructure assets and systems while sustaining an ever-increasing volume of trade with ports around the globe. Thus, terrorists need not gain access to our territory to attack our infrastructure. The Administration is establishing joint steering committees with both Canada and Mexico to improve the security of critical physical and cyber infrastructure, and is actively pursuing necessary international cooperation to increase the security of global transportation systems and commerce.

The expertise, technology, and material needed to build the most deadly weapons known to mankind— including chemical, biological, radiological, and nuclear weapons—are proliferating. If our enemies acquire these weapons, they are likely to try to use them. The consequences of such an attack could be far more devastating than those we suffered on September 11— a chemical, biological, radiological, or nuclear terrorist attack in the United States could cause large numbers of casualties, mass psychological disruption, and contamination, and could overwhelm local medical capabilities.

CHAPTER 9
Defending against Catastrophic Threats

Currently, chemical, biological, radiological, and nuclear detection capabilities are modest and response capabilities are dispersed throughout the country at every level of government. Responsibility for chemical, biological, radiological, and nuclear surveillance as well as for initial response efforts often rests with state and local hospitals and public health agencies. Today, if a natural disaster or terrorist attack causes medical consequences that exceed local and state capabilities, the Department of Health and Human Services would coordinate the deployment of medical personnel, equipment, and pharmaceuticals among the Departments of Agriculture, Defense, Energy, Justice, Transportation, Veterans Affairs, the Environmental Protection Agency, the Federal Emergency Management Agency, General Services Administration, National Communications System, U.S. Postal Service, and the American Red Cross. While the government's collaborative arrangements have proven adequate for a variety of natural disasters, the threat of terrorist attacks using chemical, biological, radiological, or nuclear weapons with potentially catastrophic consequences demands new approaches, a focused strategy, and a new organization. Our country has already expanded capabilities and improved coordination among federal agencies, but more can be done to prepare and respond.

Major Initiatives

Prevent terrorist use of nuclear weapons through better sensors and procedures. Our top scientific priority must be preventing terrorist use of nuclear weapons. Under the President's proposal, the Department of Homeland Security will implement a new system of procedures and technologies to detect and prevent the transport of nuclear explosives toward our borders and into the United States. The Department of Homeland Security would develop and deploy new inspection procedures and detection systems against the entry of such materials at all ports of entry in the United States and at major overseas cargo loading facilities. The Department—in cooperation with the Department of Transportation, state and local governments, and the private sector—would develop additional inspection procedures and detection systems throughout our national transportation structure to detect the movement of nuclear materials within the United States. It will also initiate and sustain research and development efforts aimed at new and better passive and active detection systems.

The Departments of State, Energy, and Defense are already working with foreign states possessing nuclear programs to ensure continued strict security for the global inventory of nuclear weapons and materials, consistent with domestic and international legal obligations (including the Treaty on Non-Proliferation of Nuclear Weapons). These Departments will also work with foreign governments to improve their capabilities to detect the movement of nuclear materials or weapons and to respond appropriately. They will work with foreign governments, for example, to assess their need for enhanced radiation detection capabilities at borders, seaports, and airports and, where appropriate, will coordinate the provision of detection equipment to countries where the threat from the movement of nuclear weapons and materials is significant.

Detect chemical and biological materials and attacks. The federal government, with due attention to constraints such as the need for low operating costs, will develop sensitive and highly selective systems that detect the release of biological or chemical agents. The Environmental Protection Agency, for example, is evaluating the upgrading of air monitoring stations to allow for the detection of certain chemical, biological, or radiological substances. The federal government will also explore systems that can detect whether an individual has been immunized against a threat pathogen or has recently handled threat materials. The ability to quickly recognize and report biological and chemical attacks will minimize casualties and enable first responders to treat the injured effectively. Local emergency personnel and health providers must first be able to diagnose symptoms. In addition to existing state laws mandating the reporting of threat diseases by physicians, veterinarians, and public health laboratories, rapid diagnosis of diseases of concern and communication form the cornerstone of a robust response. The Department of Homeland Security,

National Vision

America will have a coordinated national effort to prepare for, prevent, and respond to chemical, biological, radiological, and nuclear terrorist threats to the homeland.We will seek to detect chemical, biological, radiological, or nuclear weapons and prevent their entry into the United States. If terrorists use chemical, biological, radiological, or nuclear weapons, our communities and emergency personnel will be organized, trained, and equipped to detect and identify dangerous agents, respond rapidly, treat those who are harmed, contain the damage, and decontaminate the area. Our Nation will consolidate and synchronize the disparate efforts of multiple federal entities currently scattered across several departments. Under the President's proposal, the Department of Homeland Security will unify much of the federal government's efforts to develop and implement scientific and technological countermeasures against human, animal, and plant diseases that could be used as terrorist weapons. The Department would sponsor and establish national priorities for research, development, and testing to develop new vaccines, antidotes, diagnostics, therapies and other technologies against chemical, biological, radiological, or nuclear terrorism; to recognize, identify, and confirm the occurrence of an attack; and to minimize the morbidity and mortality caused by such an attack. In addition, the federal government will set standards and guidelines for state and local chemical, biological, radiological, and nuclear preparedness and response efforts. under the President's proposal, will improve infectious disease and chemical terrorism surveillance by working with the Centers for Disease Control and Prevention (CDC) and the Department of Veterans Affairs in concert with local and state public health jurisdictions. These entities will work to develop a national system to detect biological and chemical attacks. This system will include a public health surveillance system to monitor public and private databases for indicators of biological or chemical attack. National research efforts will pay particular attention to recognizing harmful dual-use industrial chemicals.

The CDC will continue its vital role in detecting, diagnosing, and addressing bioterrorist threats. Its Epidemic Intelligence Service will be expanded and modernized to better train local and state officials in recognizing biological attacks. Under the President's proposal, the Department of Homeland Security will also provide resources to state and local jurisdictions with a population of 500,000 or more to hire skilled epidemiologists. The recently established Epidemic Information Exchange System will allow the sharing of disease information in a secure information system. Public health databases will be linked nationwide through the National Electronic Disease Surveillance System to recognize patterns of disease occurrence and to identify potential regional or national outbreaks. The Laboratory Response Network will improve laboratory technology and infrastructure to increase the speed and precision of diagnoses and confirmation of biological attacks. The Department would build the capacity to gather data from all these systems and sensors, quickly assess the extent of any attack, and recommend response options to policymakers. The Department of Homeland Security, working with the Department of Agriculture, would also strengthen our parallel system for monitoring agricultural outbreaks. Since animals can serve as important sentinels signaling a biological attack against humans or be targets themselves, the Department of Homeland Security would collaborate closely with the Department of Agriculture and the Food and Drug Administration's Food and Animal Health program.

Improve chemical sensors and decontamination techniques. Private industry and the military routinely use sensors that can detect and identify toxic chemicals. Sensors with medical applications have also reached the market. Affordable, accurate, compact, and dependable sensors, however, are not available. The Department of Homeland Security would therefore fund and coordinate a national research program to develop, test, and field detection devices and networks that provide immediate and accurate warnings. The Department would also support research into decontamination technologies and procedures. As discussed in the *Emergency Preparedness and Response* chapter, the Department of Homeland Security and the Environmental Protection Agency would require assessment technologies to determine when to permit individuals to re-enter buildings and areas.

Develop broad spectrum vaccines, antimicrobials and antidotes.

In many cases, our medical countermeasures cannot address all possible biological agents or may not be suitable for use by the general population. The Departments of Health and Human Services and Homeland Security, and other government and private research entities, will pursue new defenses that will increase efficacy while reducing side effects. For example, they will explore the utility of attenuated smallpox vaccines and of existing antivirals modified to render those vaccines more effective and safe. Furthermore, the federal government, in collaboration with the private sector, will research and work toward development of broad spectrum antivirals to meet the threat of engineered pathogens aimed at both humans and livestock.

Short-and long-term efforts will expand the inventory of diagnostics, vaccines, and other therapies such as antimicrobials and antidotes that can mitigate the consequences of a chemical, biological, radiological, or nuclear attack. Development of safer smallpox vaccines and antiviral drugs will lower the risk of adverse reactions experienced with the traditional vaccine. The goal of protecting a diverse population of all ages and health conditions requires a coordinated national effort with a comprehensive research and development strategy and investment plans.

Harness the scientific knowledge and tools to counter terrorism. We will harness America's resources to fight against the most pressing chemical, biological, radiological, or nuclear challenges. In consultation with the Department of Health and Human Services, the Department of Homeland Security would leverage the expertise of America's cutting-edge medical and biotechnological infrastructure to advance the state of knowledge in infectious disease prevention and treatment, forensic epidemiology, and microbial forensics. Substantial research into relevant medical sciences is necessary to better detect, diagnose, and treat the consequences of chemical, biological, radiological, or nuclear attacks. The President has proposed a National Biological Weapons Analysis Center in the Department of Homeland Security to address some of these issues and conduct risk assessments. This Center, with input from the public health sector, will identify the highest priority threat agents to determine which countermeasures require priority research and development. The federal government will also consider and address the potential impact of genetic engineering on the biological threat. The Food and Drug Administration (FDA) ensures the availability of medical products (drugs, vaccines, and devices) in the event of the intentional use of chemical, biological, radiological, or nuclear agents. Recently, the FDA adjusted its new drug and biological product regulations so that certain human drugs designed for emergency responses can be quickly introduced based on animal rather than human tests.

Implement the Select Agent Program. Research laboratories can also counter bioterrorism through prevention, and by tracking and securing dangerous biological agents. Under the President's proposal, the Department of Homeland Security will oversee the Select Agent Program to regulate the shipment of certain hazardous biological organisms and toxins. Through the registration of more than 300 laboratories, the Select Agent Program has significantly increased oversight and security of pathogens that could be used for bioterrorism. The CDC is also training public health officials in every state to assist in accurately interpreting biosafety containment provisions and select agent procedures.

We must prepare to minimize the damage and recover from any future terrorist attacks that may occur despite our best efforts at prevention. Past experience has shown that preparedness efforts are key to providing an effective response to major terrorist incidents and natural disasters. Therefore, we need a comprehensive national system to bring together and command all necessary response assets quickly and effectively. We must equip, train, and exercise many different response units to mobilize for any emergency without warning. Under the President's proposal, the Department of Homeland Security, building on the strong foundation already laid by the Federal Emergency Management Agency (FEMA), will lead our national efforts to create and employ a system that will improve our response to all disasters, both manmade and natural.

CHAPTER 10
Emergency Preparedness and Response

Many pieces of this national emergency response system are already in place. America's first line of defense in the aftermath of any terrorist attack is its first responder community—police officers, fire-fighters, emergency medical providers, public works personnel, and emergency management officials. Nearly three million state and local first responders regularly put their lives on the line to save the lives of others and make our country safer. These individuals include specially trained hazardous materials teams, collapse search and rescue units, bomb squads, and tactical units. In a serious emergency, the federal government augments state and local response efforts. FEMA, which under the President's proposal will be a key component of the Department of Homeland Security, provides funding and command and control support.

A number of important specialized federal emergency response assets that are housed in various departments would also fall under the Secretary of Homeland Security's authority for responding to a major terrorist attack. Because response efforts to all major incidents entail the same basic elements, it is essential that federal response capabilities for both terrorist attacks and natural disasters remain in the same organization. This would ensure the most efficient provision of federal support to local responders by preventing the proliferation of duplicative "boutique" response entities. Americans respond with great skill and courage to emergencies. There are, however, too many seams in our current response plans and capabilities. Today, at least five different plans—the Federal Response Plan, the National Contingency Plan, the Interagency Domestic Terrorism Concept of Operations Plan, the Federal Radiological Emergency Response Plan, and a nascent bioterrorism response plan—govern the federal government's response. These plans and the government's overarching policy for counterterrorism are based on a distinction between "crisis management" and "consequence management." In addition, different organizations at different levels of the government have put in place different incident management systems and communications equipment. All too often, these systems and equipment do not function together well enough.

We will enhance our capabilities for responding to a terrorist attack all across the country. Today, many geographic areas have little or no capability to respond to a terrorist attack using weapons of mass destruction. Even the best prepared states and localities do not possess adequate resources to respond to the full range of terrorist threats we face. Many do not yet have in place mutual aid agreements to facilitate cooperation with their neighbors in time of emergency. Until recently, federal support for domestic preparedness efforts has been relatively small and disorganized, with eight different departments and agencies providing money in a tangled web of grant programs.

Major Initiatives

Integrate separate federal response plans into a single alldiscipline incident management plan. Under the President's proposal, the Department of Homeland Security will consolidate existing federal government emergency response plans into one genuinely all-discipline, all-hazard plan—the Federal Incident Management Plan—and thereby eliminate the "crisis management" and "consequence management" distinction. This plan would cover all incidents of national significance, including acts of bioterrorism and agroterrorism, and clarify roles and expected contributions of various emergency response bodies at different levels of government in the wake of a terrorist attack. The Department of Homeland Security would provide a direct line of authority from the President through the Secretary of Homeland Security to a single on-site federal coordinator. The single federal coordinator would be responsible to the President for coordinating the entire federal response. Lead agencies would maintain operational control over their functions (for example, the FBI will remain the lead agency for federal law enforcement) in coordination with the single on-site federal official. The Department would direct the Domestic Emergency Support Team, nuclear incident response teams, National Pharmaceutical Stockpile, and National Disaster Medical System, as well as other assets.

Create a national incident management system. Under the President's proposal, the Department of Homeland Security, working with federal, state, local, and nongovernmental public safety organizations, will build a comprehensive national incident management system to respond to terrorist incidents and natural disasters. The Department would ensure that this national system defines common terminology for all parties, provides a unified command structure, and is scalable to meet incidents of all sizes. The federal government will encourage state and local first responder organizations to adopt the already

National Vision

We will strive to create a fully integrated national emergency response system that is adaptable enough to deal with any terrorist attack, no matter how unlikely or catastrophic, as well as all manner of natural disasters. Under the President's proposal, the Department of Homeland Security will consolidate federal response plans and build a national system for incident management. The Department would aim to ensure that leaders at all levels of government have complete incident awareness and can communicate with and command all appropriate response personnel.Our federal, state, and local governments would ensure that all response personnel and organizations—including the law enforcement, military, emergency response, health care, public works, and environmental communities—are properly equipped, trained, and exercised to respond to all terrorist threats and attacks in the United States. widespread Incident Management System by making it a requirement for federal grants. All state and local governments should create and regularly update their own homeland security plans, based on their existing emergency operations plans, to provide guidance for the integration of their response assets in the event of an attack. The Department of Homeland Security will, under the President's proposal, provide support (including model plans) for these efforts and will adjust the Federal Incident Management Plan as necessary to take full advantage of state and local capabilities. State and local governments should also sign mutual aid agreements to facilitate cooperation with their neighbors in time of emergency. Starting in Fiscal Year 2004, the Department would provide grants in support of such efforts.

Improve tactical counterterrorist capabilities. With advance warning, we have various federal, state, and local response assets that can intercede and prevent terrorists from carrying out attacks. These include law enforcement, emergency response, and military teams. In the most dangerous of incidents, particularly when terrorists have chemical, biological, radiological, or nuclear weapons in their possession, it is crucial that the individuals who preempt the terrorists do so flawlessly, no matter if they are part of the local SWAT team or the FBI's Hostage Rescue Team. It is also crucial that these individuals be prepared and able to work effectively with each other and with other specialized response personnel. Finally, these teams and other emergency response assets must plan and train for the consequences of failed tactical operations. The Department of Homeland Security, as the lead federal agency for incident management in the United States, will, under the President's plan, establish a program for certifying the preparedness of all civilian teams and individuals to execute and deal with the consequences of such counterterrorist actions. As part of this program, the Department would provide partial grants in support of joint exercises between its response assets and other government teams. (This program would be voluntary for assets outside of the Department of Homeland Security.)

Enable seamless communication among all responders. In the aftermath of any major terrorist attack, emergency response efforts would likely involve hundreds of offices from across the government and the country. It is crucial for response personnel to have and use equipment, systems, and procedures that allow them to communicate with one another. Under the President's proposal, the Department of Homeland Security will work with state and local governments to achieve this goal.

In particular, the Department would develop a national emergency communication plan to establish protocols (i.e., who needs to talk to whom), processes, and national standards for technology acquisition. The Department would, starting with Fiscal Year 2003 funds, tie all federal grant programs that support state and local purchase of terrorism-related communications equipment to this communication plan and require all applicants to demonstrate progress in achieving interoperability with other emergency response bodies.

Prepare health care providers for catastrophic terrorism. Our entire emergency response community must be prepared to deal with all potential hazards, especially those associated with weapons of mass destruction. Under the President's proposal, the Department of

Homeland Security, working with the Departments of Health and Human Services and Veterans Affairs, will support training and equipping of state and local health care personnel to deal with the growing threat of chemical, biological, radiological, and nuclear terrorism. It would continue to fund federal grants to states and cities for bioterrorism preparedness. It would use the hospital preparedness grant program to help prepare hospitals and poison control centers to deal specifically with biological and chemical attacks and to expand their surge capacity to care for large numbers of patients in a mass-casualty incident. These efforts would enhance training between public health agencies and local hospitals and seek improved cooperation between public health and emergency agencies at all levels of government.

A major act of biological terrorism would almost certainly overwhelm existing state, local, and privately owned health care capabilities. For this reason, the federal government maintains a number of specialized response capabilities for a bioterrorist attack. The National Disaster Medical System, a federal/private partnership that includes the Departments of Health and Human Services, Defense, Veterans Affairs, and FEMA, provides rapid response and critical surge capacities to support localities in disaster medical treatment. Under the President's proposal, the Department of Homeland Security will assume authority over the System as part of the federal response to incidents of national significance. The System is made up of federal assets and thousands of volunteer health professionals that are organized around the country into a number of specialty teams such as Disaster Medical Assistance Teams, National Medical Response Teams, and teams trained in caring for psychological trauma. In addition, the Department of Veterans Affairs operates a vast health care, training, and pharmaceutical procurement system with facilities in many communities nationwide. The Department of Defense provides specialized skills and transportation capabilities to move these teams and evacuate casualties.

The Department of Homeland Security, working with the Department of Health and Human Services, would lead efforts to test whether illnesses or complaints may be attributable to chemical, biological, radiological, or nuclear exposure; establish disease/exposure registries; and develop, maintain, and provide information on the health effects of hazardous substances. The Environmental Protection Agency will continue to provide a laboratory diagnostic surge capacity for environmental samples during crises.

Augment America's pharmaceutical and vaccine stockpiles. The National Pharmaceutical Stockpile ensures America's ability to respond rapidly to a bioterrorist attack or a mass casualty incident. This program, which the Department of Homeland Security will operate in consultation with the Department of Health and Human Services under the President's proposal, maintains twelve strategically located "Push Packs" containing 600 tons of antibiotics, antidotes, vaccines, bandages, and other medical supplies. The federal government can transport these packs to an incident site in less than 12 hours for rapid distribution by state and local authorities. This system performed extremely well in the aftermath of the September 11 attacks, delivering a "Push Pack" to New York City in seven hours. Additional deployments followed the anthrax attacks of October 2001.

The National Pharmaceutical Stockpile already contains a sufficient antibiotic supply to begin treatment for 20 million persons exposed to anthrax and should contain enough smallpox vaccine for every American by the end of 2002. The Department of Homeland Security, working with the Department of Health and Human Services, would provide grants to state and local governments to plan for the receipt and distribution of medicines from the Stockpile. In addition, the Departments of Homeland Security and Health and Human Services would pursue accelerated FDA approval of safe and effective products to add to the Stockpile and the development of procedures to accelerate the availability of investigational drugs during a public health emergency.

Prepare for chemical, biological, radiological, and nuclear decontamination. The Department of Homeland Security would ensure the readiness of our first responders to work safely in an area where chemical, biological, radiological, or nuclear weapons have been used. The Department would begin requiring annual certification of first responder preparedness to handle and decontaminate any hazard. This certification process would also verify the ability of state and local first responders to work effectively with related federal support assets.

Under the President's proposal, the Department of Homeland Security will help state and local agencies meet these certification standards by providing grant money (based on performance) for planning and equipping, training, and exercising first responders for chemical, biological, radiological and nuclear attacks. It would launch a national research and development effort to create new technologies for detection and clean-up of such attacks. After a major incident, the Environmental Protection Agency will be responsible for decontamination of affected buildings and neighborhoods and providing advice and assistance to public health authorities in determining when it is safe to return to these areas.

Plan for military support to civil authorities. The armed forces were an integral part of our national response to the terrorist attacks of September 11. The Department of Defense currently uses a "Total Force" approach to fulfill its missions overseas and at home, drawing on the strengths and capabilities of active-duty, reserve, and National Guard forces. In addition to response from the active-duty forces, Air National Guard fighters took to the air on September 11 to establish combat air patrols. New Jersey and New York guardsmen and Navy and Marine Corps reservists provided medical personnel to care for the injured, military police to assist local law enforcement officials, key asset protection, transportation, communications, logistics, and a myriad of other functions to support recovery efforts in New York City. Maryland Army National Guard military police units were brought on duty and dispatched to provide security at the Pentagon. President Bush asked governors to call up over seven thousand National Guard personnel to supplement security at the Nation's 429 commercial airports. Guardsmen also reinforced border security activities of the Immigration and Nationalization Service and the U.S. Customs Service.

The importance of military support to civil authorities as the latter respond to threats or acts of terrorism is recognized in Presidential decision directives and legislation. Military support to civil authorities pursuant to a terrorist threat or attack may take the form of providing technical support and assistance to law enforcement; assisting in the restoration of law and order; loaning specialized equipment; and assisting in consequence management.

In April 2002, President Bush approved a revision of the Unified Command Plan that included establishing a new unified combatant command, U.S. Northern Command. This Command will be responsible for homeland defense and for assisting civil authorities in accordance with U.S. law. As in the case with all other combatant commanders, the commander of Northern Command will take all operational orders from and is responsible to the President through the Secretary of Defense. The commander of Northern Command will update plans to provide military support to domestic civil authorities in response to natural and man-made disasters and during national emergencies. The Department of Homeland Security and the Department of Defense would participate as appropriate in homeland security training that involves military and civilian emergency response personnel.

Build the Citizen Corps. Under the President's proposal, the Department of Homeland Security will maintain and expand Citizens Corps, a national program to prepare volunteers for terrorism-related response support. If we can help individual citizens help themselves and their neighbors in the case of a local attack, we will improve our chances to save lives. (See *Organizing for a Secure Homeland* chapter for additional discussion.)

Implement the First Responder Initiative of the Fiscal Year 2003 Budget. Before September 11, the federal government had allocated less than $1 billion since 1995 to help prepare first responders for terrorist attacks. A range of federal departments provided funding for training and equipment, technical assistance, and other support to assist state and local first responders. These disparate programs were a step in the right direction but fell short in terms of scale and cohesion. In January 2002, President Bush proposed the First Responder Initiative as part of his Fiscal Year 2003 Budget proposal. The purpose of this initiative is to improve dramatically first responder preparedness for terrorist incidents and disasters. This program will increase federal funding levels more than tenfold (from $272 million in the pre-supplemental Fiscal Year 2002 Budget to $3.5 billion in Fiscal Year 2003). Under the President's Department of Homeland Security proposal, the new Department will consolidate all grant programs that distribute federal funds to state and local first responders.

Build a national training and evaluation system. The growing threat of terrorist attacks on American soil, including the potential use of weapons of mass destruction, is placing great strains on our Nation's system for training its emergency response personnel. The Department of Homeland Security will under the President's proposal launch a consolidated and expanded training and evaluation system to meet the increasing demand. This system would be predicated on a four phased approach: requirements, plans, training (and exercises), and assessments (comprising of evaluations and corrective action plans). The Department would serve as the central coordinating body responsible for overseeing curriculum standards and, through regional centers of excellence such as the Emergency Management Institute in Maryland, the Center for Domestic Preparedness in Alabama, and the National Domestic Preparedness Consortium, for training the instructors who will train our first responders. These instructors would teach courses at thousands of facilities such as public safety academies, community colleges, and state and private universities. Under the President's proposal, the Department of Homeland Security will establish national standards for emergency response training and preparedness. These standards would provide guidelines for the vaccination of civilian response personnel against certain biological agents. These standards would also require certain coursework for individuals to receive and maintain certification as first responders and for state and local governments to receive federal grants. The Department would establish a national exercise program designed to educate and evaluate civilian response personnel at all levels of government. It would require individuals and government bodies to complete successfully at least one exercise every year. The Department would use these exercises to measure performance and allocate future resources.

Enhance the victim support system. The United States must be prepared to assist the victims of terrorist attacks and their families, as well as other individuals affected indirectly by attacks. Under the President's proposal, the Department of Homeland Security will lead federal agencies and provide guidance to state, local, and volunteer organizations in offering victims and their families various forms of assistance including: crisis counseling, cash grants, low-interest loans, unemployment benefits, free legal counseling, and tax refunds. In the case of a terrorist attack, the Department would coordinate the various federal programs for victim compensation and assistance, including the Department of Justice's Office for Victims of Crime and FEMA's Individual Assistance programs. (See *Costs of Homeland Security* chapter for additional discussion.)

Throughout this Nation's history we have used our laws to promote and safeguard our security and our liberty. The law will both provide mechanisms for the government to act and define the appropriate limits of that action. The President, recognizing this, directed the Office of Homeland Security to review state and federal legal authorities pertinent to homeland security. We have already taken important steps to protect our homeland. The USA PATRIOT Act, signed into law by the President on October 26, 2001, has improved government coordination in law enforcement, intelligence gathering, and information-sharing.

The Aviation and Transportation Security Act, which established the Transportation Security Administration, has strengthened civil aviation security. The Enhanced Border Security and Visa Entry Reform Act will reinforce border security systems. Finally, the Public Health Security and Bioterrorism Preparedness and Response Act will better the Nation's ability to prevent, prepare for, and respond to bioterrorism. But more needs to be done. On June 18, 2002, the President provided Congress with proposed legislation to establish a Department of Homeland Security. This new Cabinet agency would have a single, urgent mission: securing the homeland of America and protecting the American people from terrorism. Yet creation of this department does not in and of itself constitute a sufficient response to the terrorist threat. We must pass complementary legislation to address innate deficiencies in our overall ability to counter terrorism.

CHAPTER 11
Law

Where new legislation at the federal level is necessary to accomplish our counterterrorism goals, we should work carefully to ensure that newly crafted federal laws do not preempt state law unnecessarily or overly federalize counterterrorism efforts. The Tenth Amendment makes clear that each state retains substantial independent power with respect to the general welfare of its populace. States should avail themselves to the resources and expertise offered by their sister states and federal counterparts. Informed by these concepts, the *National Strategy for Homeland Security* outlines several legislative actions. This section does not purport to constitute a complete survey of needed legislative changes. Rather, the actions outlined below are initial steps in an ongoing effort to identify legislative reforms and redundancies with respect to homeland security.

Major Initiatives (Federal)

Enable critical infrastructure information sharing. Homeland security officials need quick, complete access to information relevant to the protection of physical and cyber critical infrastructure. We must meet this need by narrowly limiting public disclosure of such information in order to facilitate its voluntary submission without compromising the principles of openness that ensure government accountability. To this end, the Attorney General will convene a panel with representatives of state attorneys general, state governors, state legislators, state law enforcement, the FBI, the Environmental Protection Agency, the Department of Health and Human Services, and other federal agencies as necessary upon consultation with the Office of Management and Budget, to propose needed legislative reform or guidance regarding statutes governing public disclosure.

Streamline information sharing among intelligence and law enforcement agencies. Homeland security requires improved information sharing between the intelligence community, law enforcement agencies, and government decision-makers. Our current shortcoming in this area stems, in part, from the number of laws, regulations, and guidelines controlling intelligence operations. Congress, with the enactment of the USA PATRIOT Act, took important steps toward identifying and removing some barriers to the exchange of intelligence. The Administration will expand on this initiative by leading a review of all authorities governing the analysis, integrity, and disclosure of intelligence with the aim of improving information sharing through legislative reform while guarding against incursions on liberties.

Expand existing extradition authorities. The war on terrorism is and must be a global effort. Our country must continue to work cooperatively with nations around the world. To that end, the Departments of State and Justice should work with Congress to amend current extradition laws in two respects. First, new legislation should be adopted that would authorize extradition for additional crimes where the United States already has an extradition treaty, but where the treaty applies only to a limited set of crimes. Second, Congress should grant authority to extradite individuals from the United States for serious crimes in the absence of an extradition treaty, on a case-by-case basis with the approval of the Attorney General and the Secretary of State.

Review authority for military assistance in domestic security. Federal law prohibits military personnel from enforcing the law within the United States except as expressly authorized by the Constitution or an Act of Congress. The threat of catastrophic terrorism requires a thorough review of the laws permitting the military to act within the United States in order to determine whether domestic preparedness and response efforts would benefit from greater involvement of military personnel and, if so, how.

Revive the President's reorganization authority. Only Congress can create a new department of government; the President, however, is tasked with running the departments. Recognizing the need for flexible Presidential management authority, Congress in 1932, provided the President with the ability to reorganize the executive branch for the purpose of reducing

National Vision

We are a Nation built on the rule of law, and we will utilize our laws to win the war on terrorism while always protecting our civil liberties. We should use our federal immigration laws and customs regulations to protect our borders and ensure uninterrupted commerce; we should strengthen state codes to protect our public welfare; we should employ local, state, and federal criminal justice systems to prosecute terrorists; and we should engage our partners around the world in countering the global threat of terrorism through treaties and mutually supporting laws. Where we find our existing laws to be inadequate in light of the terrorist threat, we should craft new laws carefully, never losing sight of our strategic purpose for waging this war—to provide security and liberty to our people. We should guard scrupulously against incursions on our freedoms, recognizing that liberty cannot exist in the absence of governmental restraint. As we move forward in the fight, we should refrain from instituting unnecessary laws, as we remain true to our principles of federalism and individual freedom,. expenditures and increasing efficiency. This authority, which has taken various forms over the years, lapsed in 1984.While this Administration's priority is working with Congress to restructure the federal government to create the Department of Homeland Security, reviving the reorganization authority would greatly assist Presidents in years to come to eliminate redundancies within executive agencies and address homeland security more efficiently and economically. Congress should amend Chapter 9 of Title 5 of the U.S. Code to reinvigorate the President's authority to reorganize the executive branch.

Provide substantial management flexibility for the Department of Homeland Security. Terrorists are opportunistic, agile, and driven. In order to respond to them effectively, the Secretary of the new Department of Homeland Security must have the advantage of modern management techniques. Therefore, the Administration's proposed legislation for the Department includes 21st-century approaches to personnel and procurement policies. It also requests broad reorganization authority to enhance operational effectiveness as needed.With these and other flexible practices, the Secretary would have the managerial freedom necessary to accomplish not only the Department's primary mission of homeland security but also the important agency functions it will absorb which are not directly related to homeland security.

Major Initiatives (State)

Given the states' major role in homeland security, and consistent with the principles of federalism inherent to American government, the following initiatives constitute suggestions, not mandates, for state initiatives.

Coordinate suggested minimum standards for state driver's licenses. The licensing of drivers by the 50 states, the District of Columbia, and the United States territories varies widely. There are no national or agreed upon state standards for content, format, or license acquisition procedures. Terrorist organizations, including Al-Qaeda operatives involved in the September 11 attacks, have exploited these differences. While the issuance of driver's licenses falls squarely within the powers of the states, the federal government can assist the states in crafting solutions to curtail the future abuse of driver's licenses by terrorist organizations.

Therefore, the federal government, in consultation with state government agencies and nongovernmental organizations, should support state-led efforts to develop suggested minimum standards for driver's licenses, recognizing that many states should and will exceed these standards.

Enhance market capacity for terrorism insurance. The need for insurance coverage for terrorist events has increased dramatically. Federal support is clearly critical to a properly functioning market for terrorism insurance; nonetheless, state regulation will play an integral role in ensuring the adequate provision of terrorism insurance. To establish a regulatory approach which enables American businesses to spread and pool risk efficiently, states should work together and with the federal government to find a mutually acceptable approach to enhance market capacity to cover terrorist risk.

Train for prevention of cyber attacks. State and local officials have requested federal training regarding the identification, investigation, and enforcement of cyberrelated crimes and terrorism. The FBI, in coordination with other relevant federal organizations, should assist state and local law enforcement in obtaining training in this area.

Suppress money laundering. Terrorists use unregulated financial services, among other means, to fund their operations. The Money Laundering Suppression Act (P.L. 103-325) urges states to enact uniform laws to license and regulate certain financial services. The USA PATRIOT Act also relies on state law to establish the regulatory structure necessary to combat money laundering. States should assess the current status of their regulations regarding non-depository providers of financial services and work to adopt uniform laws as necessary to ensure more efficient and effective regulation. By doing so, states would protect consumers by providing increased stability and transparency to an industry prone to abuse while at the same time providing state and local law enforcement with the tools necessary to dismantle informal and unlicensed money transmission networks.

Ensure continuity of the judiciary. In the aftermath of a terrorist attack, our judicial system must continue to operate effectively. Planning is critical to this continuity. As such, states, relevant non-governmental organizations, and representatives of the Department of Justice and the federal judiciary should convene a committee of representatives to consider the expedient appointment of judges; interaction and coordination among federal and state judiciaries; and other matters necessary to the continued functioning of the judiciary in times of crisis.

Review quarantine authority. State quarantine laws — most of which are over 100 years old—fail to address the dangers presented by modern biological warfare and terrorism. States, therefore, should update quarantine laws to improve intrastate response while working with their sister states and federal regulators to assure compliance with minimum public health standards. To facilitate this process, the Departments of Homeland Security, Health and Human Services, Justice, and Defense should participate in a review of quarantine statutes and regulations in conjunction with state and local authorities to establish minimum standards. In addition, legislators should provide strong federal, state, and local evacuation authority through appropriate legislation or regulation.

The Nation's advantage in science and technology is a key to securing the homeland. New technologies for analysis, information sharing, detection of attacks, and countering chemical, biological, radiological, and nuclear weapons will help prevent and minimize the damage from future terrorist attacks. Just as science and technology have helped us defeat past enemies overseas, so too will they help us defeat the efforts of terrorists to attack our homeland and disrupt our way of life.

CHAPTER 12
Science and Technology

The Nation needs a systematic national effort to harness science and technology in support of homeland security. Our national research enterprise is vast and complex, with companies, universities, research institutes, and government laboratories of all sizes conducting research and development on a very broad range of issues. Guiding this enterprise to field important new capabilities and focus new efforts in support of homeland security is a major undertaking. The Department of Homeland Security, which under the President's proposal will serve as the federal government's lead for this effort, will work with private and public entities to ensure that our homeland security research and development are of sufficient size and sophistication to counter the threat posed by modern terrorism.

The private sector has the expertise to develop and produce many of the technologies, devices, and systems needed for homeland security. The federal government needs to find better ways to harness the energy, ingenuity, and investments of private entities for these purposes. Many businesses that could play a role in homeland security research and development are unaccustomed to working with the federal government and some avoid it entirely due to onerous contracting and oversight requirements. In addition, the government currently has very few programs that solicit research and development proposals focused specifically on developing new homeland security capabilities. The Department of Homeland Security would take the lead in overcoming these obstacles. The President has proposed to consolidate most of the federal government's homeland security research and development efforts under the coordination of the Department of Homeland Security to ensure strategic direction and avoid duplication. To date, research and development activities in support of homeland security have been underfunded, evolutionary, short-term in nature, fragmented across too many departments, and heavily reliant on spin-offs from the national security and medical sectors. Many of the involved agencies have little frontline knowledge of homeland security and little or no experience in technology acquisition and supporting research. The new Department would be responsible for overcoming these shortfalls by ensuring the pursuit of research and development activities where none existed previously.

The President's Fiscal Year 2003 Budget request proposed a significant increase in homeland security research and development funding: from nearly $1 billion in Fiscal Year 2002 to about $3 billion, with the bulk focused on developing new countermeasures to bioterrorism. This is a crucial first federal step for dealing with one of our most pressing scientific challenges. The Department must build on this down payment to create and implement a long-term research and development plan that includes investment in potentially revolutionary capabilities.

Major Initiatives

Develop chemical, biological, radiological, and nuclear countermeasures. The Nation's research and development agenda will prioritize efforts to deal with catastrophic threats. Key initiatives will include research and development to prevent terrorist use of nuclear weapons, detect chemical and biological materials and attacks, develop high-efficacy vaccines and antivirals against biological agents, and track laboratory use of biological agents. (See *Defending against Catastrophic Threats* chapter for additional discussion.)

Develop systems for detecting hostile intent. Terrorism ultimately requires individual human beings to carry out murderous actions. These individuals, whether they intend to commandeer an aircraft, detonate a suicide bomb, or sneak illicit material through customs, may behave in a manner that reveals their criminal intent. The Department of Homeland Security would work with private and public entities to develop a variety of systems that highlight such behavior and can trigger further investigation and analysis of suspected individuals. This would allow security officials at points of interest such as airports and borders to examine more closely individuals who exhibit such characteristics and also have other indications of potentially hostile intent in their background. The Department would also explore whether appropriate sensors can determine whether individuals have been immunized or otherwise exposed to biological agents, chemical agents, or nuclear materials.

Apply biometric technology to identification devices. As our military, intelligence, and law enforcement efforts in Afghanistan and other countries have demonstrated, bringing justice to terrorists and their supporters is complicated by the fact that they hide among innocent civilians and in remote places. Finding terrorists and preventing terrorist attacks here in the United States is difficult for the same reason—for example, a terrorist on the FBI's Watch List may sneak past security personnel at an airport thanks to false documents and a simple disguise. These challenges require new security actors. We will explore both evolutionary improvements to current capabilities and development of revolutionary new capabilities. The Department of Homeland Security will ensure appropriate testing and piloting of new technologies. Finally, the Department, working with other agencies, will set standards to assist the acquisition decisions of state and local governments and private-sector entities.

National Vision

In the war on terrorism, America's vast science and technology base provides a key advantage. With the Department of Homeland Security as a focal point, the United States will press this advantage through a national research and development enterprise for homeland security similar in emphasis and focus to that which has supported the national security community for more than fifty years. The Department will establish a disciplined system to guide its homeland security research and development efforts and those of other departments and agencies. As a Nation, we will emphasize science and technology applications that address catastrophic threats. We will build on existing science and technology whenever possible. We will embrace science and technology initiatives that can support the whole range of homeland technologies and systems to identify and find individual terrorists. The Department of Homeland Security would support research and development efforts in biometric technology, which shows great promise. The Department would focus on improving accuracy, consistency, and efficiency in biometric systems. Furthermore, the Department would explore biomolecular and other new techniques, as well as enhancements to current techniques such as noise suppression methods for voice authentication.

Improve the technical capabilities of first responders. If we do not protect our first responders from the dangerous effects of chemical, biological, radiological, and nuclear attacks, we may lose the very people we depend on to minimize the damage of any such attacks. The Department of Homeland Security would launch a steady and long-term effort to provide first responders with technical capabilities for dealing with the effects of catastrophic threats—capabilities that would aid both first responders and victims of the attack. These capabilities would include protective gear and masks, prophylactic treatments, and decontamination equipment. The Department would undertake sustained efforts to develop treatments and decontamination methodologies for radiological and nuclear events. The Department would also focus on developing new methods to merge disparate databases and provide first responders with accurate and usable pictures of building layouts and other key information about the site of a terrorist incident. In all these efforts, the Department would pay great attention to ensuring that these technologies are easy to use under the extreme conditions in which first responders operate.

Coordinate research and development of the homeland security apparatus. The Department of Homeland Security, working with the White House and other federal departments, would set the overall direction for our Nation's homeland security research and development. The Department would establish a management structure to oversee its research and development activities and to guide its interagency coordination activities. It would base these efforts on a constant examination of the Nation's vulnerabilities, continual testing of our security systems, and updated evaluations of the threat and its weaknesses. It would make sure that new technologies can scale appropriately —in terms of complexity, operation, and sustainability—to meet any terrorist attack, no matter how large.

The technologies developed through this research and development should not only make us safer, but also make our daily lives better; while protecting against the rare event, they should also enhance the commonplace. Thus, the technologies developed for homeland security should fit well within our physical and economic infrastructure and our national habits. System performance must balance the risks associated with the terrorist threat against the impact of false alarms and impediments to our way of life.

Establish a national laboratory for homeland security. Under the President's proposal, the Department of Homeland Security will establish a laboratory—actually a network of laboratories—modeled on the National Nuclear Security Administration laboratories that provided expertise in nuclear weapon design throughout the Cold War. These laboratories would provide a multidisciplinary environment for developing and demonstrating new technologies for homeland security and would maintain a critical mass of scientific and engineering talent with a deep understanding of the various operational and technical issues associated with homeland security systems. The Department would establish a central management and research facility with satellite centers of excellence located at various national laboratories.

The national laboratory for homeland security would develop, demonstrate, and then transition to the field new technologies and system concepts to counter the specific threats of chemical, biological, radiological, and nuclear terrorism. It would transfer successful technologies to commercial industry for manufacture and long-term support. It would reach out to various regional, state, and local homeland security efforts, gaining familiarity with their issues, and providing them core research, development, test, and evaluation expertise. The laboratory would help the Department of Homeland Security's efforts to conduct and support threat and vulnerability analyses.

Solicit independent and private analysis for science and technology research. Under the President's proposal, the Department of Homeland Security will fund independent analytic support for our homeland security science and technology endeavors. These efforts will support planning activities, including net assessment, preparing agency guidance, and reviewing agency programs and budgets; systems analyses; requirements analyses; assessments of competing technical and operational approaches; and the Department's use of "red team" techniques. (See *Intelligence and Warning* chapter for additional details on "red team" techniques.) The organizations that provide this support to the Department will undertake long-range projects and should have access to sensitive government and proprietary data, including intelligence assessments. They should also possess unquestionable objectivity, staying free from conflicts of interest with other government institutions and the private sector.

Establish a mechanism for rapidly producing prototypes. Technologies developed for a variety of purposes are often directly applicable, or quickly adaptable, for homeland security needs. Under the President's proposal, the Department of Homeland Security will work with other federal agencies to provide a means for rapid prototyping of innovative homeland security concepts based on existing technologies. It would collect unsolicited ideas, evaluate them, and maintain a capability for funding the most promising ideas either directly or in partnership with a relevant agency. The Department would ensure that successful prototypes are sustainable by partnering with the commercial sector for manufacture and long-term support.

Conduct demonstrations and pilot deployments. The Department of Homeland Security would systematically engage in pilot deployments and demonstrations to provide a conduit between the state and local users of technology and the federal developers of that technology. These pilot deployments and demonstrations would serve as a focal point for the development of regional solutions, testing how well new homeland security technologies work under local conditions across America. We must also test how well those technologies work in the case of a large-scale attack.

Set standards for homeland security technology. In order to encourage investment in homeland security science and technology efforts, the Department of Homeland Security, along with other federal agencies, would work with state and local governments and the private sector to build a mechanism for analyzing, validating, and setting standards for homeland security equipment. The Department would develop comprehensive protocols for certification of compliance with these standards. This activity will allow state and local officials to make informed procurement decisions.

Establish a system for high-risk, high-payoff homeland security research. Bringing the full force of science to bear on our efforts to secure the homeland will require systematic investment in innovative and revolutionary research and development projects. We expect many of these projects to fail due to the technical risks involved, but the payoff for success will be great. The Department of Homeland Security would establish a program with a high level of programmatic and budgetary flexibility to solicit private industry for innovative concepts.

Through these and other focused science and technology programs, we will develop new tools and techniques to secure our homeland. Our enemies are adaptive, constantly searching for new ways to strike us.We must do the same. Just as we did in World War II and in the Cold War, we must use our great strength in science and technology to triumph in the war on terrorism.

CHAPTER 13
Information Sharing and Systems

Information contributes to every aspect of homeland security and is a vital foundation for the homeland security effort. Every government official performing every homeland security mission depends upon information and information technology.

Although American information technology is the most advanced in the world, our country's information systems have not adequately supported the homeland security mission. Today, there is no single agency or computer network that integrates all homeland security information nationwide, nor is it likely that there ever will be. Instead, much of the information exists in disparate databases scattered among federal, state, and local entities. In many cases, these computer systems cannot share information—either "horizontally" (across the same level of government) or "vertically" (between federal, state, and local governments). Databases used for law enforcement, immigration, intelligence, and public health surveillance have not been connected in ways that allow us to recognize information gaps or redundancies. As a result, government agencies storing terrorism information, such as terrorist "watch lists," have not been able to systematically share that information with other agencies. These differences can sometimes result in errors if, for example, visa applications and border controls are not checked against consistent "watch lists." It is crucial to link the vast amounts of knowledge resident within each agency at all levels of government. Despite spending some $50 billion on information technology per year, two fundamental problems have prevented the federal government from building an efficient government-wide information system. First, government acquisition of information systems has not been routinely coordinated. Over time, hundreds of new systems were acquired to address specific agency requirements. Agencies have not pursued compatibility across the federal government or with state and local entities. Organizations have evolved into islands of technology—distinct networks that obstruct efficient collaboration. Second, legal and cultural barriers often prevent agencies from exchanging and integrating information.

Information-sharing capabilities are similarly deficient at the state and local levels. Many states maintain terrorism, gang, and drug databases that other states cannot access. In addition, there are deficiencies in the communications systems used by municipalities throughout the country. If an attack were to occur today, most state and local first responders would not be using compatible communications equipment. Wireless technology used by most communities is outdated, and one-third of public safety agencies have reported trouble communicating with counterparts during incidents (according to the Public Safety Wireless Network, a joint program of the Departments of Justice and Treasury). Although many states have instituted new infrastructures for sharing information within their jurisdiction, sharing with other states and with federal agencies remains fragmented. This lack of interoperability was evident many times over the past decade—during the 1993 World Trade Center bombing, the 1995 Oklahoma City bombing, the 1999 Columbine school shootings, and the September 11 attacks. At Columbine, the responders included 23 local and county law enforcement agencies, two state and three federal law enforcement agencies, six local fire departments, and seven local emergency medical services—most with incompatible communications procedures and equipment.

Major Initiatives

Five principles will guide our country's approach to developing information systems for homeland security. First, we will balance our homeland security requirements with citizens' privacy. Second, the homeland security community will view the federal, state, and local governments as one entity—not from the point of view of any agency or level of government. Third, information will be captured once at the source and used many times to support multiple requirements. Fourth, we will create databases of record, which will be trusted sources of information. Finally, the homeland security information architecture will be a dynamic tool, recognizing that the use of information technology to combat terrorism will continually evolve to stay ahead of the ability of terrorists to exploit our systems.

It is important to protect the public's right to access information, but to do so in balance with security concerns. In general, laws such as the Freedom of Information Act (FOIA) provide for access to government information to the extent that records are not exempt from disclosure. At the same time, Congress has crafted numerous exemptions identifying categories of information that should not be publicly disclosed as the public interest weighs against it. In making decisions about this category of information— such as whether to make it available on agency web sites—agencies must weigh the benefits of certain information to their customers against the risks that freely-available sensitive homeland security information may pose to the interests of the Nation.

Integrate information sharing across the federal government. Under the President's proposal, the Department of Homeland Security will coordinate the sharing of essential homeland security information of the personnel and resources available to address these threats. Officials will receive the information they need so they can anticipate threats and respond rapidly and effectively. The incorporation of data from all sources across the spectrum of homeland security will assist in border management, critical infrastructure protection, law enforcement, incident management, medical care, and intelligence. In every instance, sensitive and classified information will be scrupulously protected. We will leverage America's leading-edge information technology to develop an information architecture that will effectively secure the homeland.

National Vision

We will build a national environment that enables the sharing of essential homeland security information. We must build a "system of systems" that can provide the right information to the right people at all times.

Information will be shared "horizontally" across each level of government and "vertically" among federal, state, and local governments, private industry, and citizens. With the proper use of people, processes, and technology, homeland security officials throughout the United States can have complete and common awareness of threats and vulnerabilities as well as knowledge nationwide through the Critical Infrastructure Assurance Office. This would include the design and implementation of an interagency information architecture to support efforts to find, track, and respond to terrorist threats in a way that improves both the time of response and the quality of decisions. The Critical Infrastructure Assurance Office will also define pilot projects to address immediate homeland security requirements while laying the foundation for continuous improvement. New coordination groups will recommend better information-sharing methods, focusing on, among other things, border security; transportation security; emergency response; chemical, biological, radiological, and nuclear countermeasures; and infrastructure protection.

As described in the *Domestic Counterterrorism* chapter, the FBI will create a consolidated Terrorism Watch List that includes information from a variety of sources and will be fully accessible to all law enforcement officers and the intelligence community. The Department of Homeland Security, as proposed by the President, will oversee a joint project of the U.S. Customs Service, Immigration and Naturalization Service, Transportation Security Administration, and International Trade Data System Board of Directors for large-scale modernization at border crossings.

Integrate information sharing across state and local governments, private industry, and citizens. Several efforts are underway to enhance the timely dissemination of information from the federal government to state and local homeland security officials by building and sharing law enforcement databases, secure computer networks, secure video teleconferencing capabilities, and more accessible websites. First, the FBI and other federal agencies are augmenting the information available in their crime and terrorism databases such as the National Crime Information Center and the National Law Enforcement Telecommunications Systems. These databases are accessible to state and local authorities. Second, state and local governments should use a secure intranet to increase the flow of classified federal information to state and local entities. This would provide a more effective way to disseminate information about changes to the Homeland Security

Advisory System and share information about terrorists. The federal government will also make an effort to remove classified information from some documents to facilitate distribution to more state and local authorities. The effort will help state and local law enforcement officials learn when individuals suspected of criminal activity are also under federal investigation and will enable federal officials to link their efforts to investigations being undertaken in the states. The Department of Homeland Security would create a Collaborative Classified Enterprise environment to share sensitive information securely among all relevant government entities. This effort, which is to include dozens of agencies, will put in place a secure communications network to allow agencies to "plug in" their existing databases to share information.

Third, a secure video conferencing capability connecting officials in Washington, D.C. with all government entities in every state will be implemented by the end of the calendar year. This capability will allow federal officials to relay crucial information immediately to state homeland security directors and enhance consultation and coordination. Fourth, expansion of the '.gov' domain on the Internet for use by state governments has already been completed. In the past, only federal government websites were permitted to use the '.gov' domain. This change will ensure the legitimacy of government websites and enhance searches of all federal and state websites, thereby allowing information to be accessed more quickly. These '.gov' sites will also allow homeland security officials to exchange sensitive information on the secure portions of those websites.

Adopt common "meta-data" standards for electronic information relevant to homeland security. The Administration has begun several initiatives to integrate terrorist-related information from databases of all government agencies responsible for homeland security. As this information is assembled, it is crucial to compile simultaneously information about the information so that homeland security officials understand what is available and where it can be found. This complements the effort to analyze the information with advanced "data-mining" techniques to reveal patterns of criminal behavior and detain suspected terrorists before they act. The Department of Homeland Security, Department of Justice, FBI, and numerous state and local law enforcement agencies would use data-mining tools for the full range of homeland security activities.

The National Spatial Data Infrastructure (NSDI) is a working example of compiling meta-data to facilitate integration of data and support decision making. The NSDI is a network of federal, state, and local geospatial information databases that provide metadata for all information holdings to make information easier to find and use. The assembled data will include geospatial products, including geographic information systems that will be used with incident management tools and allow immediate display of maps and satellite images. The President's geospatial information integration e-government initiative will increase the amount of meta-data available on the NSDI and develop data standards that permit additional integration of information. The geospatial e-gov initiative efforts will be coordinated with incident reporting data to create real time maps and images for use across government in domestic counterterrorism and incident management.

Improve public safety emergency communications. In an emergency, rescue personnel cannot afford to be hampered by incompatible communications assets. Under the President's proposal, the Department of Homeland Security will work to develop comprehensive emergency communications systems. The National Communications System would be incorporated into the Department of Homeland Security to facilitate the effort. These systems will disseminate information about vulnerabilities and protective measures, as well as allow first responders to better manage incidents and minimize damage. The new Department would pursue technologies such as "reverse 911" which would call households to alert those at risk. Project SAFECOM, one of the President's egovernment initiatives, is being designed to address the Nation's critical public safety wireless shortcomings and will create a tactical wireless infrastructure for first responders and federal, state, and local law enforcement and public safety entities.

Ensure reliable public health information. The Department of Homeland Security, in cooperation with the Department of Health and Human Services, would also work to ensure reliable public health communications. Prompt detection, accurate diagnosis, and timely reporting and investigation of disease epidemics all require reliable communication between medical, veterinary, and public health organizations. Once an attack is confirmed it is crucial to have realtime communication with other hospitals, public health officials, other health professionals, law enforcement, emergency management officials, and the media. The Centers for Disease Control and Prevention has created the Health Alert Network to increase the interconnectivity of federal, state, and local public health and emergency response agencies for timely communications about health advisories, laboratory findings, information about disease outbreaks, and distance learning. Under this plan, 90 percent of every state will be covered by this highspeed network and the capacity to receive emergency broadcast health alert messages. Providing the public timely and accurate risk communication during a public health emergency will inform as well as reassure concerned Americans.

CHAPTER 14
International Cooperation

In a world where the terrorist pays no respect to traditional bound-aries, a successful strategy for homeland security requires international cooperation. America must pursue a sustained, steadfast, and systemat-ic international agenda to counter the global terrorist threat and improve our homeland security. This agenda lies at the nexus of the *National Strategy for Homeland Security* and the *National Security Strategy of the United States.*

Following September 11, the United States began a campaign to engage our partners around the globe in the fight against terrorism. We have made significant progress. We have built international support for action against global terrorism. We have entered into cooperative efforts to improve security against terrorist attacks on the United States. We have, for example, made arrangements with Canada and Mexico to improve the security of our shared land borders. Similarly, we are working with partners around the world to improve the security of inter-national commerce and transportation networks to prevent their exploitation by terrorists. And we have embarked upon joint scientific technological research and development aimed at countering the many dimensions of the terrorist threat. Our global engagement to secure the homeland intersects with our government's efforts in other areas as well. Consequently, some initiatives will be closely coordinated, and even shared, between the *National Strategy for Homeland Security* and our other national strategies, especially the *National Security Strategy of the United States,* the *National Strategy for Combating Terrorism*, and the *National Strategy to Combat Weapons of Mass Destruction.* Oversight of such initiatives— which include international law enforcement and intelligence cooperation and the protection of critical infrastructure networks—will be shared between our government's homeland security and national security structures to reduce seams in our defenses that may be exploited by our enemies.

Major Initiatives

Create "smart borders." The United States is working closely with its neighbors to improve efforts to stop terrorists and their instruments of terror from entering the United States. The United States has entered into "Smart Border" agreements with Mexico and Canada to meet this objective. (See *Border and Transportation Security* chapter for additional discussion.)

Combat fraudulent travel documents. More than 500 million people cross our borders every year. Verifying that each has a legitimate reason to enter the United States requires international support. The United States is working with the G-8 group of nations, the International Civil Aviation Organization, and other entities to set improved security standards for travel documents such as passports and visas. The Department of State, working with the Department of Homeland Security, will negotiate new international standards for travel documents by the earliest possible date. The United States will launch a pilot program with select countries to share information about specific incidents of travel document fraud and illegal entry and deportation.

Increase the security of international shipping containers. Sixteen million containers enter our Nation every year. The United States will work with our trade partners and international organizations to identify and screen high-risk containers and develop and use smart and secure containers. (See *Border and Transportation Security* chapter for additional discussion.)

Intensify international law enforcement cooperation. Since September 11, the U.S. government has worked with individual countries and through multilateral international organizations to improve cooperation on law enforcement action against terrorists. These efforts have focused on freezing the assets of terrorists and affiliated persons and organizations.We have also worked together to prevent terrorist recruitment, transit, and safe haven, and have cooperated with other countries to bring terrorists to justice.

The Department of Justice, in cooperation with the Department of State, will continue to work with its foreign counterparts on law enforcement issues. The FBI headquarters will build closer working relationships with foreign counterparts on counterterrorism matters through its new Flying Squads. (See *Domestic Counterterrorism* chapter for additional discussion.) The United States will continue to press its G-8 counterparts for implementation of the 25-point Counterterrorism Action Plan approved at the November 2001 joint meeting of the G-8 Lyon Group (International Crime Experts Group) and Roma Group (Counterterrorism Experts Group).

Help foreign nations fight terrorism. The U.S. government provides other countries with specialized training and assistance to help build their capacities to combat terrorism. Some of these programs are military in nature, but many focus on improving the efforts of civilian authorities. They range from seminars in drafting legislation to the provision of equipment for enhancing border security and customs capabilities.

Expand protection of transnational critical infrastructure. The United States will continue to work with both Canada and Mexico to improve physical and cyber security of critical infrastructure that overlaps with both countries. (See *Protecting Critical Infrastructure and Key Assets* chapter for additional discussion.)

National Vision

The United States will work with traditional allies and new friends to win the war on terrorism. We will sustain a high level of international commitment to fighting terrorism through global and regional organizations (such as the United Nations and the Organization of American States), major international fora (such as the G-8), specialized organizations (such as the World Health Organization, the International Civil Aviation Organization, and the International Maritime Organization), multilateral and bilateral initiatives, and, where needed, new coordination mechanisms. We will work with our neighbors and key trading partners to create systems that allow us to verify the legitimacy of people and goods entering our country. We will increase information sharing between law enforcement, intelligence, and military organizations to improve our collective ability to counter terrorists everywhere, including in America. We will increase international cooperation on scientific and technological research designed to help prevent, protect against, and respond to terrorist threats and attacks. We will work with our partners to prepare to support one another in the wake of any attack. As we implement this *Strategy* we will be sensitive to treaty and other obligations; however, where we find existing international arrangements to be inadequate or counterproductive to our efforts to secure our homeland, we will work to refashion them. Throughout these efforts, we will harmonize our homeland security policies with our other national security goals.

Amplify international cooperation on homeland security science and technology. In addition to our national program to develop and deploy new technologies and new uses of technology against terrorism, the U.S. government will encourage and support complementary international scientific initiatives. For example, the United States will seek to establish cooperative endeavors with Canada and Mexico for cross-border efforts to detect biological weapons attacks; eventually, these programs may be expanded to include other friendly nations. In conjunction with the Department of State and the intelligence community, the Department of Homeland Security would also work with certain close allies to improve techniques and develop new technologies for detecting hostile intent.

Improve cooperation in response to attacks. The United States will continue to work with other nations to ensure smooth provision of international aid in the aftermath of terrorist attacks. The Department of State, working closely with the Department of Homeland Security and others, will lead these efforts. The United States will expand its exercise and training activities with Canada in 2003 as part of the Smart Border Initiative. It will establish similar activities with Mexico. It will also initiate bilateral and multilateral programs to plan for efficient burden sharing between friendly nations in the case of attack. For example, the United States will work with its NATO allies to outline the organization's role in preventing and responding to terrorist attacks on member states.

Review obligations to international treaties and law. The United States is party to all 12 counterterrorism instruments adopted by the United Nations in recent years. These treaties form an important part of our multilateral counterterrorism strategy. We are actively encouraging all United Nations members to join and fully implement all 12 conventions. On a bilateral basis, the United States will negotiate and renegotiate, if appropriate, mutual legal assistance treaties (MLATs) based on U.S. law enforcement priorities that will help advance homeland security. MLATs allow the exchange of evidence in a form usable at trial. MLATs also enable law enforcement to obtain information abroad in connection with the investigation, prosecution, and prevention of offenses in a manner that is more speedy, efficient, and reliable than the traditional judicial letters rogatory process.

CHAPTER 15
Costs of Homeland Security

The national effort to enhance homeland security will yield tremendous benefits and entail substantial financial and other costs. The benefit will be a reduction in both the risk of future terrorist events and their consequences should an attack occur. The financial costs are the amount of money, manpower, equipment, and innovative potential that must be devoted to homeland security—resources which then cannot be used for goods, services, and other productive investments. Americans also incur substantial costs in longer delays at airport security checkpoints and restrictions on some individual freedoms. While these costs are often difficult to measure quantitatively, they are no less real and burdensome to Americans. We must measure and balance both benefits and costs to determine the correct level of homeland security efforts. This chapter describes the broad principles that should guide the allocation of financial resources for homeland security, help determine who should bear the financial burdens, and help measure the costs. The

United States spends roughly $100 billion per year on homeland securi-
ty. This includes the services of federal, state, and local law enforcement
and emergency services but excludes most spending for the armed
forces. The cost is great, and we will strive to minimize the sacrifices
asked of Americans, but as a Nation we will spend whatever is necessary to secure the homeland.

Principles to Guide Allocation of Homeland Security Costs
Balancing benefits and costs. Decisions on homeland security activities
and spending must achieve two overarching goals: to devote the right
amount of scarce resources to homeland security and to spend these
resources on the right activities. To achieve the first goal, we must carefully weigh the benefit of each homeland security endeavor and only
allocate resources where the benefit of reducing risk is worth the
amount of additional cost. One implication of this standard is that it is
not practical or possible to eliminate all risks. There will always be
some level of risk that cannot be mitigated without the use of unaccept-
ably large expenditures. The second goal for homeland security spending is to prioritize those activities that most require additional
resources. Given the resources available, we should strive to maximize
security by distributing additional funding in such a way that the value
added is approximately equal in each sector. Because some activities
might achieve substantial benefits at low cost, while others result in
minimal gain at a high price, resources should be shifted to their most
"productive" use. These shifts should continue until the additional value
of risk mitigation per dollar is equalized.

The role for government. The government should only address
those activities that the market does not adequately provide—for example, national defense or border security. Our government provides these
services on behalf of American citizens for our collective benefit. Many
homeland security activities—such as a national incident management
system—require government action.

For other aspects of homeland security, sufficient incentives exist
in the private market to supply protection. In these cases, we should rely
on the private sector. For example, owners of large buildings and hosts
of large events may have a sufficient incentive to provide security for
those venues.

Federalism and cost sharing of expenditures. The homeland security mission requires a national effort— federal, state, and local govern-

ments partnering together and with the private sector. It is critical that we identify tasks that are most efficiently accomplished at the federal versus local or regional level. A central criterion is the degree to which the activity is national or sub-national in scope. Many homeland security activities, such as intelligence gathering, border security, and policy coordination, are best accomplished at the federal level. In other circumstances, such as with first responder capabilities, state and local governments are better positioned to handle these responsibilities.

At a time when budgets are tight across the country, the federal government will play a key role in securing the homeland. It is critical, however, that all levels of government work cooperatively to shoulder the costs of homeland security. The federal government will lead the effort, but state and local governments can and should play important roles. As a result, Americans will gain from these homeland security efforts every day with improvements in public services such as law enforcement and public health systems.

Regulations. Traditionally, governments have used regulations in addition to direct expenditures to meet their objectives. Rigid regulation, however, has proven to be an inefficient means of meeting objectives. To the extent that homeland security objectives are to be met by regulations for state and local governments or private-sector firms, the federal government will provide an incentive to minimize costs and reward innovation by permitting maximum flexibility in meeting those objectives. The federal government will focus on specifying outcomes rather than the means by which they will be achieved.

The Costs of Homeland Security

Homeland security requirements take real resources (such as labor, capital, technology, and managerial expertise) away from valued economic activities (such as household consumption or business investment). In some cases, homeland security spending also reduces resources that could be used to purchase other types of public safety, such as cleaner water or safer highways. In other cases, the investment in homeland security will result in public safety benefits; water testing to detect chemical or biological agents, for example, will improve overall water quality. The sum of these economic resources shifted toward homeland security is the fundamental economic cost of the endeavor.

Direct federal expenditure. In recent years, the federal government has allocated considerable resources to homeland security. Including supplemental funding, the federal budget allocated $17 billion to home-land security in Fiscal Year 2001. This amount increased to $29 billion in Fiscal Year 2002. In Fiscal Year 2003, the President budgeted $38 bil-lion for homeland security activities. These budget allocations must be viewed as down payments to cover the most immediate security vulner-abilities.

The President has noted that terrorism is the greatest national secu-rity threat since World War II. Minimizing the overall economic impact of fighting the war on terrorism will require that increased budgetary spending on homeland security occur within the context of overall fis-cal spending restraint. It is important to reprioritize spending to meet our homeland security needs, and not simply to permit unchecked over-all growth in federal outlays. Over the long term, government spending is balanced by either higher taxes or inflation, both of which hinder the rapid economic growth that serves as the ultimate source of resources for families' standards of living and national needs.

If we do not reprioritize spending, then the costs of homeland secu-rity will be even greater because these expenditures do not represent the full cost of homeland security to the economy. As noted earlier, the $38 billion in taxes needed to finance the Fiscal Year 2003 homeland secu-rity budget request will not be available for other uses such as personal consumption and private sector investments. The Council of Economic Advisers estimates that of the $38 billion, $24 billion would come from reduced consumption, while $14 billion would take the form of reduced private sector investment. The cost is even higher, however, because of the economic distortions introduced by the tax system. Under any tax system, every dollar collected in taxes results in distortions that reduce the efficiency of the economy and lower national income. This eco-nomic distortion (referred to as deadweight loss) is roughly $0.27 per dollar of tax revenue.

State and local governments. It is difficult to measure the financial contributions to homeland security made by state and local govern-ments. It is evident, however, that state and local governments are spending money or planning to spend money which was never expected to be spent on defending and protecting their respective communities. These costs include protecting critical infrastructure, improving tech-nologies for information sharing and communications, and building emergency response capacity. At this time, the National Governors' Association estimates that additional homeland security-related costs, incurred since September 11 and through the end of 2002, will reach approximately $6 billion. Similarly, the U.S. Conference of Mayors has estimated the costs incurred by cities during this time period to be $2.6 billion.

Private expenditures. Private businesses and individuals have incentives to take on expenditures to protect property and reduce liability that contribute to homeland security. Owners of buildings have a significant stake in ensuring that their buildings are structurally sound, properly maintained, and safe for occupants. To accomplish this, they often take protective measures that include employee education and training, securing services, infrastructure assessment, technology, and communication enhancements. Properly functioning insurance markets should provide the private sector with economic incentives to mitigate risks.

Costs of homeland security in the private sector are borne by both the owners of businesses in the form of lower income and their customers in the form of higher prices. The Council of Economic Advisers estimates that private business spent approximately $55 billion per year on private security before the September 11 attacks. As a result of the attacks, their annual costs of fighting terrorism may increase by 50 to 100 percent. Increases in the cost of insurance premiums have been more dramatic.

Economic Recovery

Additional homeland security costs would be incurred in the event of a terrorist attack. The economic response and recovery efforts would involve four central activities.

Local economic recovery. The federal government is developing a comprehensive and coordinated economic recovery plan. The plan will improve federal support to state and local governments for incidents that overwhelm state, local, and private-sector resources. This approach will help develop a better planned and more flexible federal response, support stronger local planning for economic recovery, lessen federal demands on state and local officials at the time of an incident, and provide federal assistance to state and local bodies, when appropriate, in a more user-friendly and effective way.

Restoration of financial markets. In the aftermath of an attack, the Department of Homeland Security, the Department of the Treasury, and the White House would oversee efforts to: effectively monitor financial market status; identify and assess impacts on the markets from direct or indirect attacks; develop appropriate responses to such impacts; inform senior federal officials of the nature of the incident and the appropriate response options; and implement response decisions through appropriate federal, state, local, and private sector entities.

National economic recovery. A major terrorist incident can have economic impacts beyond the immediate area. Therefore, the Departments of Homeland Security, Treasury, and State and the White House would identify the policies, procedures and participants necessary to assess economic consequences in a coordinated and effective manner. This group will develop recommendations to senior federal officials on the appropriate federal response. The group will ensure that government actions after an attack restore critical infrastructure, services, and our way of life as quickly as possible and minimize economic disruptions. This group will also develop effective policies and procedures for the implementation of those responses through appropriate federal, state, local, and private sector bodies.

Economic impact data. Sound information about the nature and extent of the economic impact of an incident is important in developing an effective response. The Department of Commerce's Economics and Statistics Administration and other federal agencies are developing an economic monitoring, assessment, and reporting protocol to provide credible information concerning the economic status of the area before an incident, assess the direct economic impacts of the incident, and estimate the total economic consequences in a more timely and accurate manner. This protocol will help develop more accurate national, regional, and local economic impact data. This information will be provided to appropriate government officials to help assess the appropriate response to the economic consequences of an incident.

CHAPTER 16
Conclusion: Priorities for the Future

This *National Strategy for Homeland Security* has set a broad and complex agenda for the United States. The *Strategy* has defined many different goals that need to be met, programs that need to be implemented, and responsibilities that need to be fulfilled. The principal purpose of a strategy, however, is to set priorities. It is particularly important for government institutions to set priorities explicitly, since these institutions generally lack a clear measure of how successfully they provide value to the citizenry.

Setting priorities is important to homeland security in two distinct respects. First, there is the question of the priority of homeland security compared to everything else the government does or might do. There is a strong consensus that protecting the people from terrorist attacks of potentially catastrophic proportions is among the highest, if not the highest, priority any government can have. There will, of course, be vigorous debate over how to achieve specific homeland security goals, who should pay, how much security is enough, and what the responsibilities of different entities should be, but there is little disagreement that securing the homeland is more important than just about every other government activity.

Second, there is the more complex question of priorities within the

homeland security agenda. This point is absolutely essential in determining how to allocate the taxpayers' money in a government budget.
The President's Budget for Fiscal Year 2003, which was finalized in the
weeks immediately following September 11 and submitted to Congress
in February 2002, recognized the need for priorities. It identified four
key areas for extra attention and carefully targeted increases in federal
expenditures:

Support first responders. The President's 2003 budget request
included $3.5 billion to enhance first responders' response capabilities
in communities across the Nation. These funds will support states and
communities as they conduct exercises, purchase equipment, and train
personnel.

Defend against biological terrorism. The 2003 budget request
proposed increasing, by $4.5 billion to $5.9 billion total, spending on
programs that counter the threat of biological terrorism. Areas of
emphasis include: improving disease surveillance and response systems; increasing the capacity of public-health systems to handle outbreaks of contagious diseases; expanding research on vaccines, medicines, and diagnostic tests; and building up the National
Pharmaceutical Stockpile.

Secure America's borders. The Administration proposed increasing spending on border security by $2.2 billion to $11 billion in 2003.
These funds will expand the number of inspectors at ports of entry; purchase equipment to increase inspections of containers and cargo; design
and test a statutorily required system that records the entry of individuals into the United States and their subsequent exit; and improve the
Coast Guard's ability to track maritime activity.

Use information to secure the homeland. The 2003 budget proposed an increase in spending of $722 million on programs that will use
information technology to more effectively share information and intelligence horizontally (between federal agencies) and vertically (between
federal, state, and local governments). These initiatives are the
President's budgetary priorities for Fiscal Year 2003, and will remain
important issues for the foreseeable future.

There is, however, an additional statutory and institutional priority
at the present time—namely, the establishment of the new Department
of Homeland Security as proposed by the President on June 6, 2002.
Congress is considering legislation to implement the President's pro-

posal even as this *National Strategy* is being published. Building a strong, flexible, and efficient Department of Homeland Security is an enormous challenge and a top federal priority. Assuming Congress passes legislation to implement the President's proposal to create the Department of Homeland Security, the budget will fully reflect the reformed organization of the executive branch for homeland security. The Fiscal Year 2004 Budget will also have an integrated and vastly simplified account structure based on the six critical mission areas defined by the *National Strategy*.

Indeed, work has already begun on the Fiscal Year 2004 budget. At the time this *National Strategy* was published, it is expected that in Fiscal Year 2004 the Administration will attach priority to the following items.

Enhance the analytic capabilities of the FBI (p. 17). The first objective of this strategy is to prevent terrorist attacks. The FBI is among the most important federal institutions for achieving this objective. The FBI is seeking to enhance its analytic capabilities to support counterterrorism investigations and operations, as well as to enhance the counterterrorism capabilities of other components of the federal government.

Build new capabilities through the Information Analysis and Infrastructure Protection Division of the proposed Department of Homeland Security (p. 18). Under the President's proposal, the Department of Homeland Security will build on capabilities to comprehensively assess the vulnerabilities of our critical infrastructure and key assests, map threats against those vulnerabilities, issue timely warnings, and work with federal, state, and local governments and the private sector to take appropriate protective action.

Create "smart borders" (p. 22). We must prevent terrorists and the implements of terror from entering the United States. At the same time, our economic security depends on the efficient flow of people, goods, and services. We will build a "smart border" that achieves both of these critical goals. It will feature strong, advanced risk-management systems, increased use of biometric identification information, and partnerships with the private sector to allow precleared goods and persons to cross borders without delay.

Increase the security of international shipping containers (p. 23). Ensuring the security of the global trading system is essential to our security and world commerce. Some 16 million shipping containers enter the United States each year; roughly two-thirds come from 20 "mega" seaports. The United States will work with its trade partners to increase security in these ports, establish greater controls over containers, pre-screen containers before they arrive in America, and develop technologies to track in-transit containers.

Recapitalize the U.S. Coast Guard (p. 23). The President is committed to building a strong and effective Coast Guard. The Administration's Fiscal Year 2004 Budget proposal will provide resources to acquire the sensors, command-and-control systems, shore-side facilities, boats and cutters, aircraft, and people the Coast Guard 68 THE NATIONAL STRATEGY FOR HOMELAND SECURITY requires to perform all of its missions, including assuring the safety of Americans at sea, maritime domain awareness, and fisheries enforcement.

Prevent terrorist use of nuclear weapons through better sensors and procedures (p. 38). The federal government will support research efforts for improved technologies to detect nuclear materials and weapons. In particular, the Department of Homeland Security would develop and deploy new detection systems and inspection procedures against the entry of such materials at all major ports of entry and throughout our national transportation infrastructure.

Develop broad spectrum vaccines, antimicrobials, and antidotes (p. 39). The Department of Homeland Security and the Department of Health and Human Services would support research efforts to expand the inventory of diagnostics, vaccines, antidotes, and other therapies that can mitigate the consequences of a chemical, biological, radiological, or nuclear attack. Protecting a diverse population of all ages and health conditions requires a coordinated national effort with a comprehensive research and development strategy and investment plans. Such efforts will also benefit other infectious disease and medical research.

Integrate information sharing across the federal government (p. 56). The federal government will develop systems to coordinate the sharing of essential homeland security information. The federal government will design and implement an interagency information architecture that will support efforts to find, track, and respond to terrorist threats in a way that improves both the time of response and the quality of decisions. These items will be the budgetary priorities of the federal government for the next budget cycle. In the intervening months, the executive branch will prepare detailed implementation plans for these and most other initiatives contained within this *Strategy*. These plans will ensure that the taxpayers' money is spent only in a manner that achieves specific objectives with clear performance-based measures of effectiveness. State and local governments, private industry, and concerned citizens groups should go through a similar process of priority-setting and long-term planning.

 * * * Americans will never forget the murderous events of September 11, 2001. Our Nation suffered great harm on that terrible morning. The American people have responded magnificently with courage and compassion, strength and resolve. There should be no doubt that we will succeed in weaving an effective and permanent level of security into the fabric of a better, safer, stronger America.

ACRONYMS

APHIS: Animal and Plant Health Inspection Service

ATSA: Aviation and Transportation Security Act

ATTF: Anti-Terrorism Task Force

CBRN: Chemical, Biological, Radiological and Nuclear

CDC: Center for Disease Control

CIA: Central Intelligence Agency

CIAO: Critical Infrastructure Assurance Office

CTC: Counter-Terrorism Center

DCI: Director of Central Intelligence

DHS: Department of Homeland Security (proposed)

DoD: Department of Defense

DoE: Department of Energy

EIS: Epidemic Intelligence Service

EPA: Environmental Protection Agency

FAA: Federal Aviation Administration

FBI: Federal Bureau of Investigation

FDA: Food and Drug Administration

FEMA: Federal Emergency Management Agency

FTTTF: Foreign Terrorist Tracking Task Force

HAN: Health Alert Network

HHS: Health and Human Services

HSTF: Homeland Security Task Force (proposed)

IIPO: Information Integration Program Office

IMS: Incident Management System

INS: Immigration and Naturalization Service

ITDS: International Trade Data System

JTTF: Joint Terrorism Task Force

MRC: Medical Reserve Corps

MLAT: Mutual Legal Assistance Treaty

NCIC: National Crime Information Center

NCS: National Communication System

NDMS: National Disaster Medical System

NEDSS: National Electronic Disease Surveillance System

NIH: National Institutes of Health

NLETS: National Law Enforcement Telecommunications System

NRC: Nuclear Regulatory Commission

NSA: National Security Agency

NSC: National Security Council

NSDI: National Spatial Data Infrastructure

NWP: Neighborhood Watch Program

OHS: Office of Homeland Security

OMB: Office of Management and Budget

TIPS: Terrorism Information and Preventive Systems

TSA: Transportation Security Administration

TSWG: Technical Support Working Group

VIPS: Volunteers in Police Service

WMD: Weapons of Mass Destruction

WTC: World Trade Center

SEPTEMBER 11 AND AMERICA'S RESPONSE

The American people responded to the attacks of September 11 with compassion and resolve. Virtually every American participated in one way or another in helping our Nation recover and grow stronger. Some rushed into burning buildings to save the lives of colleagues, friends, and strangers. Others demonstrated their solidarity by wearing an American flag on their lapel. Members of our military flew combat air patrols over our cities; some fought overseas. Many people ministered to the injured and comforted the grieving, while others worked in their official capacities—as legislators, policymakers, investigators, prosecutors, first responders, health officials, environmental experts, counselors, and economists—to help America recover from the attacks and confront the terrorist threat. People in every state, every city, and every government agency have contributed to the effort to make America safer. Our efforts so far have created the solid foundation on which we continue to build our defenses. While the work to protect Americans and our way of life will continue indefinitely, we as a country can be comforted by our knowledge that the work is well underway. Highlighted below are a few of the many actions taken by our Nation since September 11.

The Immediate Response to the Attacks *Rescue, recovery, and victim support.* The response to the September 11 terrorist attacks began onboard the hijacked planes as passengers did all they could to thwart the terrorists, and continued in the streets of New York City, in the rubble of the Pentagon, and in the burning Pennsylvania countryside. Colleagues assisted each other in escaping from the collapsing buildings. Firefighters, police officers, emergency medical professionals, and public works employees responded immediately to the crime scenes, while hospitals treated the many victims. The recovery and clean-up efforts involved significant contributions from all sectors of our society—federal, state, and local agencies and entities, the private sector, volunteer organizations, as well as individual citizens. The work to help the recovery effort and to assist the victims of September 11 did not stop at Ground Zero. It continued as Congress and the President worked to appropriate $40 billion in emergency funds to compensate victims, aid the reconstruction efforts in New York and Virginia, and strengthen our fight against terrorism. In addition, the American response persisted in the board rooms of private companies and charitable organizations as various sectors worked to raise money and donate supplies to aid the victims.

The investigation. In response to September 11, the U.S. government initiated the largest criminal investigation in our Nation's history, committing more than 4,000 FBI agents and 3,000 support staff to the effort. The investigation has been supported by numerous federal agencies, as well as state and local law enforcement.

While the investigation has been led by law enforcement, significant contributions have come from many sectors. For example, Congress and the President, by passing and signing into law the USA PATRIOT Act, provided law enforcement with the tools necessary to bring the guilty to justice. In addition, the international community joined us in the global war on terrorism, enabling law enforcement to investigate groups and terrorist cells throughout the world. The American population helped as well, by providing law enforcement with important investigatory leads, calling the Justice Department's hotline to report suspected terrorist activity, and logging onto the web site created so that people could share information.

After September 11, the federal government committed not only to rooting out terrorists wherever they are, but also to cutting off their sources of financial support. To support this effort, and to identify and eliminate funding sources of suspected terrorists, the Treasury Department launched Operation Green Quest at the U.S. Customs

Service and the FBI established the Financial Review Group. Within weeks of September 11, the President issued an Executive Order to starve terrorists of their support funds. To date, the United States has blocked $34.3 million in assets of suspected terrorist organizations and terrorist supporters/financiers. The global effort of more than 160 countries has resulted in the freezing of over $112 million in assets.

The Response to the Terrorist Threat Federal, state, and local governments and the private sector must coordinate on issues affecting homeland security in order to succeed in the fight against terrorism.

Officials across all levels of government have been working together on homeland security related task forces to meet this goal. In addition, each state now has a designated individual, charged by the respective Governor, to perform homeland security responsibilities. The private sector has also worked closely with the government and with one another to better secure the homeland. For example, the Business Roundtable, an organization of Fortune 100 companies, established CEO COM Link, the Critical Emergency Operations Communication Link, to quickly alert and mobilize America's business leaders in times of national crisis or a natural disaster. Working closely with government officials, the Grocery Manufacturers of America launched Project Vigilance—a program that encompasses a task force on food security, "twenty-four, seven" databases, and other food industry actions to help assure the security of food and consumer products.

Supporting first responders. The members of the Nation's emergency services community are our first responders to terrorist attacks. Americans have done a great deal since September 11 to support our firefighters, police officers, emergency personnel, and other responders. In the wake of the attacks, many cities reviewed and made changes to their emergency plans. Congress appropriated $650 million for federal grant assistance to states and localities for improving first responder terrorism preparedness. With this vital federal assistance, first responders have received and will continue to receive extensive training (including in weapons of mass destruction response) and necessary equipment.

Americans in their private capacities have joined in supporting our emergency personnel as well. The President created USA Freedom Corps to strengthen and expand opportunities to protect our homeland, as well as to support our communities and to extend American compassion around the world. As part of this initiative, Citizen Corps offers a wide range of volunteer opportunities to support first responders through its five national level programs. To name just one example, the Federal Emergency Management Agency's Community Emergency Response Team program—part of Citizen Corps—trains volunteers to help support first responders during an incident. (See *Organizing for a Secure Homeland* chapter for additional discussion and description of Citizen Corps programs.)

Critical infrastructure and key asset protection. Our Nation's efforts to protect against the terrorist threat have included increased security of our country's critical infrastructure and key assets. This increased security has taken many forms—heightened patrols, threat assessments, access restrictions—and has been undertaken by many agencies at all levels of government. For example, the Department of Defense has flown more than 22,000 combat air patrol missions within the United States since September 11 to protect our critical infrastructure from air attacks. The Nuclear Regulatory Commission (NRC) placed nuclear power plants across the Nation on the highest level of security after the attacks, while the U.S. Customs Service placed the Nation's air, land, and sea ports of entry on Alert 1 Level, ensuring more thorough examinations of people and cargo. In addition, the NRC initiated a top-to-bottom security review of nuclear power plants, including an assessment of plant vulnerability to aircraft.

Yet the federal government has not acted alone in protecting our physical infrastructure. States and cities have also increased security at critical sites. In Jonesboro, Arkansas, the police department has concentrated security into areas that traditionally did not receive much attention, directing patrols for communication towers, water storage and treatment facilities. Local law enforcement coordinated with the Coast Guard to create a safety zone around Indian Point Energy Center, located 50 miles from New York City. Utah, with federal assistance, instituted flight and satellite surveillance over reservoirs. In Fresno, California, the police department staffed an antiterrorism unit that conducted a survey of city buildings and security readiness. In Tampa, Florida, marine, air, and uniform patrols have been instituted at an important port, while in Wellington, Florida, new security measures have been installed in a water treatment plant.

The private sector, which owns the majority of our infrastructure, has also increased its security of its facilities. For example, the National Food Processors Association formed the Alliance for Food Security almost immediately after September 11 to better protect the food supply from intentional contamination. The American Chemistry Council's emergency communication center joined with the FBI's Hazardous Materials Response Team shortly after September 11, augmenting and improving their information- sharing and coordination activities. In addition to our physical infrastructure, all levels of government, as well as private entities, have taken measures to increase the security of our critical computer and information infrastructure. The President's Critical Infrastructure Protection Board has spurred research into potential methods to protect vital communications networks. The U.S. government established stronger encryption standards to safeguard sensitive, non-classified electronic information. The state legislatures of Louisiana, Michigan, and the Commonwealth of Virginia have passed cyberterrorism laws.

The attacks on the World Trade Center and on the Pentagon starkly illustrated the need to protect our transportation systems, among other critical infrastructures, from acts of terrorism. Accordingly, more than 7,000 members of the National Guard, and later thousands of state and local law enforcement personnel, were deployed to help secure the Nation's airports. Congress passed the Aviation and Transportation Security Act, which established a series of challenging milestones to achieve a secure air travel system. The Federal Air Marshals program was substantially expanded and new security procedures have been implemented at the Nation's 429 commercial airports.

Cities and states have also committed energy and resources to protecting our means of transportation, and across the country, local law enforcement and state governments have dedicated more hours, money, and personnel to securing modes of transportation. For example, in West Virginia state employees patrolled the state's highways, bridges, and waterways, while the City of Chicago increased security at its bridges and airports. States, including New Jersey, North Carolina, and Virginia, have also taken measures to increase security relating to driver's licenses by changing the requirements and identifying information necessary to obtain a license.

Protecting large events. The September 11 attacks created public concern regarding the safety of large spectator events, to which law enforcement at every level has responded with careful planning and coordination of security arrangements. The February 2002 Winter Olympic Games in Salt Lake City, Utah, were a major test of America's ability to protect a large public event. Security at Salt Lake City was more thorough, more visible, better planned, and better coordinated than at any Olympics in history. The designation of the Olympics as a National Special Security Event brought federal support to the Games in the areas of venue security, air space security, training, communications, and credentialing. Throughout the Games, federal, state, and local agencies shared intelligence to ensure a high level of readiness, and dozens of state and local law enforcement agencies took part in security planning, contributing valuable resources and invaluable expertise.

National biodefense. On the heels of the tragedies of September 11, we found ourselves under attack once again – this time from the dissemination of anthrax through the mail. These attacks illustrated the need to make prevention of and protection against bioterrorist attacks a top priority. Our country has already taken several important steps, including the procurement of 200 million doses of smallpox vaccine, and the expansion of the National Pharmaceutical Stockpile. (See *Emergency Preparedness and Response* chapter for additional discussion.)

While the federal government plays a critical role in increasing our defenses against bioterrorist attacks, state and local governments are integral to prevention as well, and they have taken action. Michigan spent $2.6 million for epidemiologists, microbiologists, and lab personnel to increase the state's ability to respond to bioterrorist attacks. The City of Baltimore created a web-based surveillance system to track the appearance of common symptoms in uncommon amounts that might indicate a biological attack.

Private industry has engaged as well. For example, four major pharmaceutical companies, using information from the Centers of Disease Control and Prevention, have begun to distribute reference guides to doctors and caregivers on how to detect and treat anthrax in patients.

Protecting our borders. Since September 11, we have taken important measures to protect our borders more effectively. The U.S. Coast Guard deployed additional personnel to protect our ports of entry immediately after the attacks, while the Immigration and Naturalization Service and the National Guard augmented their presence on our northern and southern borders. In addition, the Foreign Terrorist Tracking Task Force has been working to bar terrorists or terrorist-supporting aliens from the United States and to track down and deport any who have illegally entered the United States.

We need the help of our closest neighbors—Mexico and Canada—to fully protect our borders. In December 2001, the United States and Canada concluded a "Smart Border Declaration," which committed our governments to working together to build a secure border that operates efficiently and effectively under all circumstances. The U.S. and Canadian governments have already made great strides in realizing that vision, aggressively implementing a detailed 30-point action plan of specific measures to securely facilitate the free flow of people and commerce.

In a similar fashion, the United States and Mexico signed the "U.S. – Mexico Border Partnership" declaration in March 2002. Currently, border management agencies from both the United States and Mexico are working together to implement a 22-point action plan of specific measures to ensure the secure flow of legal goods and people, and to build adequate bordermanagement systems and infrastructure.

Protecting our borders involves not only knowing who enters our country, but also what comes across our borders. To protect the security of cargo entering the United States, the U.S. Customs Service launched Customs-Trade Partnership Against Terrorism. This joint initiative of the government and the private sector requires importers to take steps that will ensure tighter security of cargo, and, in return, the government agrees to give the more secure, low risk cargo the "fast lane" through our ports of entry.

Communicating with and engaging the public. The attacks of September 11 filled America with apprehension. Government representatives have worked to alleviate the anxiety in the months that have followed through responsible communication with the public. The government faces a balancing act on this front: the public's need and right to know about terrorist threats versus the risk of raising alarm unnecessarily or fruitlessly by relaying all information including ambiguous or non-specific threat information. In response to this pressing need for clear communication, and recognizing that an informed public is a key asset, the President created the Homeland Security Advisory System to provide the public with the necessary information and awareness regarding terrorist threats and protective action.

Our citizens also responded to September 11 with a dedication to overcome the terrorist threat at home. The President created the Citizen Corps initiative to offer Americans the opportunity to volunteer to protect their communities through emergency response and preparation. Public response has been impressive. More than 100 communities, ranging from major metropolitan areas to small suburban and rural communities, have formed Citizen Corps Councils to coordinate local volunteer activities to support first responders. More than 38,000 individuals from all 50 states have signed up online to participate in one or more of the federally supported Citizen Corps programs, including Volunteers in Police Service, Neighborhood Watch and Operation TIPS, sponsored by the Department of Justice; the Medical Reserve Corps, sponsored by the Department of Health and Human Services; and the Federal Emergency Management Agency's Community Emergency Response Team training.